THE
ROYAL FAMILY

THE ROYAL FAMILY

Text by
Rupert O. Matthews

Featuring the photography of
David Levenson & Glenn Harvey

This edition produced by Ted Smart for
The Book People Ltd,
Guardian House,
Godalming, Surrey GU7 2AE

ISBN 1-85613-013-4

Manufactured in Spain

Produced by Ted Smart
Text and Captions by Rupert O. Matthews
Designed by Sara Cooper
Production Assistant : Seni Glaister

Featuring the photography of

Glenn Harvey

17, 18 BL and BR, 19, 21 (4), 24 TR and B, 26/27, 28 BR, 29
(2), 30 (3), 32 (4), 33, 34 T and BL, 35, 37 BL and BR, 38, 39 BL
and BR, 41 (3), 42 T and BL, 48 TR, 49 BR, 56, 58, 59 (3), 61 T
and BL, 63, 64 T, 65 TL, 69 TR, 70 (5), 71, 72 (4), 73 (3), 74 (3),
77, 78(3), 79 TL, TR and BL, 84 T, 92 (4), 93 (4), 96 TL, TR and
BR, 97, 102 TL, BL and BR, 103 (4), 104 (4), 105, 109 (3), 119 T,
121 TR and BL, 124 (4), 125 B, 126 TL, 127 (4), 130, 131 (4),
132 TR and BR, 133 B, 134 (4), 135 TR, TL and BR, 136 (4),
137 TR and BL, 146 BL and BR, 147 BR,
148, TL, TR and BR, 149, 150 (2), 151 (4), 152 TR, CR and B,
153 (4), 156 (3), 157, 158 (3), 159 (4),

David Levenson

18 T and C, 20, 23 BR, 24 TL, 25, 28 T and BL, 31, 34 BR, 37
TL and TR, 39 TL and TR, 40 TL, TR and BL, 47 BL, 48 BL
and BR, 49 T and BL, 50 (3), 51 (2) 52/53, 54, 55 (3), 57 (3), 61
BR, 62 TL, TR and BL, 63 T, 65 BR, 68, 69 TL BL and BR, 75
(4), 76 (3), 79 BR, 80 (4), 81 (3), 82 (2), 83 T and BL, 84 BL and
BR, 85 (3), 86 BL and BR, 89 (4), 94 (3), 95 (2), 96 BL and BR,
98 (4), 99 (4), 100 (3), 101, 102 TR, 106 (4), 107 (4), 108, 110
(4), 111 (4), 112 (4), 113 (4), 114 (4), 115 (4), 116 (4), 117 (4), 118
(3), 119 B, 120, 121 BR, 123 TR, 125 T, 126 TR, BL and BR, 128
(4) 129 T and C, 132 TL and BL, 133 T, 135 BR, 137 TL and
BR, 139 (2), 140/141, 145 (2), 146 TL and TR, 147 T and Bl,
148 BL, 152 TL

Rex Features

22, 23 T and BL, 36, 40 BR, 42 BR, 43 (3), 44 (4), 45, 46, 47 T
and BR, 48 TL, 60, 61 C, 62 BR, 63 BL, 64 BL, C and BR, 65
TR and BL, 66 (4), 67, 83 BR, 86 TL and TR, 87, 88 (4), 90 (4),
91 (4) 122, 123 TL, BL and BR, 142 (4), 143 (3), 144 (4), 154,
155 (4)

Camera Press, 160
Lucy Levenson 121 TL, 129 BL and BR

The birth of a new princess is always a happy occasion, but the birth of a new daughter to the Duke and Duchess of York was even more joyful than usual. The crowds which had gathered outside the London hospital in the hope of catching a glimpse of the proud father, or of being the first to see the new arrival, littered the streets with champagne corks when the birth was announced. Even the oldest newspaper hack could not fail to be affected by the emotion which the new birth produced in the crowd of well wishers huddled together against a chill March day.

It was appropriate that the new princess, named Eugenie Victoria Helena, should be born to the Yorks, the most recently married of the Queen's immediate family. Their first child, Princess Beatrice, was only recently able to toddle about on the day her sister was born and was happily unaware of the stranger about to enter what had previously been her exclusive nursery. The Yorks were losing no time in surrounding themselves with their own little family.

The marriage, like the birth, had been accompanied by numerous popping champagne corks and numbers of well wishers on the London streets. Held on the 23rd July 1986 the marriage of Prince Andrew, Duke of York, to Miss Sarah Ferguson, as the Duchess then was, held the entire nation and much of the world spellbound. In London crowds began gathering before the first threads of dawn lightened the eastern sky over Docklands. Film crews and television cameramen began taking their places soon after breakfast. By the time the first guests made their way towards Westminster Abbey the streets were packed with vast numbers of well wishers.

The highlight for the millions watching on television came when Sarah emerged from her carriage to reveal her wedding dress. It was a stunning way for a new member of the royal family to make her appearance. The magnificent silk gown trailed a 17 foot train and was richly embroidered with pearls and sequins worked into crests and initials.

For the bride the marriage was more than a wedding, it was a commitment to join the premier family of Britain and a step into a high-profile lifestyle utterly unlike anything she had known before. The life of a royal person is not an easy one, and for the new Duchess of York the task may have seemed daunting. However, from her first appearance on the scene when an engagement between herself and Prince Andrew was first suggested in the press, she has been a popular member of the royal family.

It was as a 'Sloane Ranger' that Sarah Ferguson first came to the attention of the press. She lived in a bachelor flat with girlfriends in Lavender Gardens, in Clapham, and worked in the arts world. The engagement was announced on 19th March and the future member of the royal family moved to stay with the Queen Mother in Clarence House. The relaxed informal style of 'Fergie' as the tabloid press dubbed her, won many friends while her highly mobile and expressive face ensured that she featured constantly in the world's photographic press.

Those who feared that the demands of royalty might cause the joyful, carefree commoner to lose her obvious good humour and friendliness need not have worried. Since her marriage in 1986, the Duchess of York has shown herself to be a remarkably easy going and popular addition to the royal family. Her infectious goodwill makes the many functions she attends all the more enjoyable for her hosts or fellow guests.

In that other great prerequisite for a royal lady, taste in fashion, the Duchess has triumphed as well. Shunning the glamorous chic of the Princess of Wales, the young duchess has become famous for her more casual style of clothing. Indeed, she sometimes appears slightly ill at ease in the most formal of clothes demanded of a lady in her position and is at her best in relaxed surroundings.

The first of her fashion styles to take on in a big way was the bow. First coming in prominence at the official engagement photocall in the form of a discreet black hair clip, the bow soon established itself as a favourite accessory. On her first official engagement with Andrew, Sarah appeared in a stylishly cut leaf-green two piece suit and high-necked white blouse which were set off nicely by a huge green and black bow which held back the famous mane of red hair.

At the wedding itself the bow reached its apogee in the form of a massive silk bow where the train joined the waist. In size and position it was rather like the bustle of an Edwardian dress.

Fashion designers were not slow to spot the importance of a style set by the newest royal. Soon bows were appearing not only in fashionable boutiques but also in high street shops across the nation. There were long dresses with waistlines set off by bows, stockings with tiny bows at the heel, and hair bows by the thousand. The bow remained in style for well over a year, but eventually fell from favour as fashion moved on. The Duchess has not ceased to be a trend setter, however. Her frequent public appearances have kept her in the eye of fashion designers and of the fashion purchasers. The fact that Prince Andrew is a full-time naval officer has unavoidably cut down the number of official engagements carried out by the couple so 'Fergie's' influence on the world of fashion is not as great as it might be or, indeed, might become.

In pursuing a naval career Prince Andrew is following in the steps of his grandfather, the previous Duke of York who later became King George VI. The young Prince Albert, as the future king was then known, was the second son of the reigning monarch, as is Prince Andrew. He entered the Royal Navy at an early age. When just 21 years old Prince Albert was serving in the Grand Fleet based at Scapa Flow when, in May 1916, news came that the German High Seas Fleet had put to sea. The First World War was at its height and control of the North Atlantic was crucial. The Grand Fleet immediately steamed out to face the challenge of the German navy.

Young Prince Albert was serving as a Lieutenant on HMS *Iron Duke*, the flagship of Admiral Jellicoe. The scouting ships of the two fleets sighted each other about 2pm on 31st May and fighting broke out at once. Within a few hours the heavy ships, including HMS *Iron Duke* came into action. That the young Prince was not entirely safe on his large ship was proved when HMS *Invincible*, flagship of Admiral Hood, was shot to pieces and sunk claiming the lives of Hood and most of the crew. Indeed HMS *Iron Duke* became involved in the heaviest fighting and the young prince was officially commended for his behaviour under fire.

During the misty night contact was lost with the German fleet, which steamed to its home harbour without further action. Though the German High Seas Fleet was still largely intact after the battle it never dared put to sea again, so the Royal Navy gained the strategic victory.

The present Duke of York, like his grandfather, joined the

navy and became involved in a memorable battle before he was accorded his title on the occasion of his wedding. On 2nd April 1982 Argentinian troops invaded the Falkland Islands and a new and entirely unexpected war broke out.

Now 22 years old, Prince Andrew was a helicopter pilot on the aircraft carrier HMS *Invincible* at the time. His ship was ordered south as part of a task force to retake the islands. The Argentinian press greeted the news with the comment 'send us your little prince'. It was perhaps ominous that Prince Andrew was putting to sea in a ship which bore the same name as one his grandfather had seen blown out of the water, but few noticed the coincidence.

Tragedy almost struck on 25th May when an Exocet guided missile was spotted heading straight for HMS *Invincible*. The crew immediately fired chaff, sheets of aluminium foil, to confuse the missile's radar guidance. The ruse worked and the Exocet veered off. Unfortunately the rogue missile picked up a second target, the supply ship *Atlantic Conveyer*, which was struck and gutted beyond repair.

All this time Prince Andrew was flying his helicopter on a variety of missions. On the bleak Falkland Islands which lacked roads, or even paths, across most of their area, helicopters filled an invaluable supply role. Helicopters could carry heavy loads of ammunition and food up to front line troops in a matter of minutes, and could evacuate wounded as quickly. During such journeys, Prince Andrew would have had to dodge Argentinian ground fire and would have needed to dive for cover whenever an enemy jet came in sight. Even more hazardous was his duty of decoying enemy missiles. The trick was to position the helicopter in such a way that the homing missiles locked on to the metal of the helicopter rather than to the metal of the ship. Having successfully attracted the missile, the pilot then had to dodge it, leaving the deadly machine to fly harmlessly past.

Though he shares the naval career and title of his grandfather, Prince Andrew is in other ways very different from the previous Duke of York. In stark contrast to the slight, painfully shy George VI, Prince Andrew is large, robust and enormously outgoing. These traits became clear early in his life at the enthusiastically outdoor Scottish school Gordonstoun where he was educated. He entered the navy almost immediately on leaving school. The training as a naval officer which he underwent filled Prince Andrew out both physically and as a character in the public's eye. He rapidly became known as a good-looking and fun-loving young man who was always prepared to indulge in high-spirited episodes.

Andrew's active and dangerous role in the Falklands War brought him fresh respectability as both a man of action and a prince willing to shoulder his responsibilities. A much publicised interview in which he spoke of being 'very much on your own' when lying flat on a heaving deck with shrapnel and bullets flying around earned him further respect among those who had shared the fears and horrors of war.

It was almost inevitable that both the press and public should begin to take an increased interest in Prince Andrew after these episodes. Of perhaps the most absorbing interest was the subject of his possible future marriage. Journalists began scouring the prince's social life for a possible candidate. In October 1982 they found a subject which they considered fully deserving of their attention. In hindsight the episode seems to have been rather overplayed by the press.

The subject of the speculation was an actress named Kathleen Stark, known to her friends as Koo. She was one of several guests at Princess Margaret's holiday home on the Caribbean island of Mustique when Prince Andrew was there on two weeks leave. When a fellow holidaymaker reported that Prince Andrew's well known boisterous sense of fun had taken the form of tucking a live lobster into Koo's swimsuit, press speculation of a romance increased its pace.

The story became hotter news when details of Miss Stark's career were revealed. It was discovered that she had posed nude for photographers and had appeared in films which some considered not the most sedate ever produced. Dozens of photographers and pressmen suddenly descended on Mustique in quest of a story and soon rumours were circulating and, sometimes, being printed as fact.

It was reported that the Queen was not impressed by the media speculation. Prince Andrew came home from the holiday early and alone to return to naval duties. A few reports of clandestine meetings between the couple appeared in print over the following weeks, but the story appeared to be dying away. Immediately after Christmas, however, Koo was spotted wearing Prince Andrew's naval dog tag on a necklace and press speculation erupted once again. When nothing further occurred to fuel stories of the romance, press interest faded.

In March the press again speculated this time about a young lady named Vicki Hodge, who was part of a weekend party which included the Prince, but little more was heard of her in the press. More embarrassing for the journalists were the events of August when rumours of romance circulated about Prince Andrew and a certain 'Sophie' who had stayed at Balmoral with the prince. Press teams identified the young lady and descended on her armed with note-pads and cameras. The story appeared in several national papers, but unfortunately they had got the wrong girl. The guest was actually a friend of the Queen, not Andrew's, and nobody was even aware of any hint of romance. The journalists bowed out gracefully and left Andrew in peace for some time.

When speculation began around Sarah Ferguson it was from the start much more serious than had been the talk surrounding earlier girlfriends. It might be guessed that the romance had progressed well before it reached the newspapers.

Since his marriage, Prince Andrew seems to have settled down somewhat. His earlier high spirited attitude to the navy has been transformed into a serious career. He became qualified as aircraft commander soon after returning from the Falklands War and has since been posted to a ship as pilot of the vessel's sole helicopter, a Lynx. His wife has also learnt to fly and thus can better understand her husband's work and its demands.

If Prince Andrew is unlike his grandfather in his extrovert ways and string of alleged romances, he is also extremely unlikely to follow the previous Duke of York to the throne, unless some catastrophe occurs. George VI came the throne unexpectedly in 1936 when his elder brother King Edward VIII abdicated. The dramatic move was caused by the king's wish to marry the twice divorced American woman Wallis Simpson. When the politicians refused to accept Mrs Simpson as a suitable queen, Edward stepped down.

Prince Andrew's elder brother, Prince Charles, on the other hand has made a highly suitable marriage and has two sons, both of whom rank closer to the throne than does Prince Andrew. That Prince Andrew was not so close to the throne as had been his grandfather and great-grandfather did not come about until 1982, when Prince Charles was aged 34. Until that time there had always been the nagging worry haunting the back of people's minds that history might repeat itself and a fresh abdication crisis break out. Not only would this have proved disastrous for the Prince, it would also have been extremely serious for the royal family and its constitutional position within the nation.

Those who either knew Prince Charles or who had followed his career closely, however, would have known that such an event was extremely unlikely. It would be almost impossible to imagine a man who has taken his allotted role in life more seriously and conscientiously. There can never have been any doubt that Prince Charles would make an excellent Prince of Wales, or that in time he shall prove to be one of the finest kings of recent generations.

The first great public ceremonial at which Charles appeared in public was his mother's coronation in 1953. The young prince did not take part in the solemn proceedings. No doubt a five year old would have found the long service and seemingly endless ceremonial extremely trying and difficult. As with any youngster involved in long adult events he could have created 'a scene' and spoilt the day. Instead Charles watched the ceremony from a side aisle within Westminster Abbey. Dressed in an immaculate white outfit complete with ruffed shirt, he was seated next to his beloved grandmother, Queen Elizabeth the Queen Mother.

In the event it was as well that he was placed next to his grandmother and away from the main ceremony. Not that the young heir misbehaved in any way, but he clearly found the service somewhat trying. He often gazed around in a rather bored manner, and persistently troubled his patient companion with questions and queries after the manner of young children. He had, however, regained his composure in time for the official photographs at Buckingham Palace and for the obligatory appearance on the balcony. Here, for perhaps the first time, he was assailed by the cheers and adulation of the people and might have begun to realise exactly what his birth meant for him.

After his public appearances in coronation year, Prince Charles retreated somewhat from the public eye while he was educated for his future. All previous heirs to the throne had been educated at home by private tutors. Prince Philip, however, felt that changing times demanded changing practices and it was decided that the young heir should be sent to school. At the age of 8, therefore, Prince Charles began attending Hill House School in Knightsbridge.

Two years later he transferred to Cheam School and it was here that Prince Charles took another step forward on his path towards playing his adult role. In 1958 the Queen officially conferred the title Prince of Wales on her eldest son, though he was not expected to take the duties of the office seriously until his investiture some years later.

The title has traditionally been held by the eldest son of the reigning monarch since the 13th century. Wales had previously been made up of a number of principalities which at various times owed allegiance to each other or to England, or were independent. King Edward I of England brought all of Wales under his control and in 1284 created his son, later Edward II, Prince of Wales.

The reason for this move was twofold. First he hoped that by recognising that Wales was different from England and allowing it to follow age old customs he would ensure that the Welsh would remain content with the new regime. Secondly he knew that he had to place somebody he could trust in charge of such a powerful and turbulent area. For very much the same reasons his immediate successors also created their eldest sons Princes of Wales.

Today the title carries with it no power or wealth, but many responsibilities. Prince Charles ensures that he visits Wales regularly and often in order to emphasise his guardianship over the Principality.

Four years after being created Prince of Wales, Charles left for boarding school. Again the influence of Prince Philip can be discerned for Charles was sent to Gordonstoun, where his father had been educated. Gordonstoun is a robust outdoor school located in the Scottish mountains. The school concentrates on promoting self-confidence without arrogance, self-control without shyness and a sound all-round education. It also ran its own mountain rescue service and coastguard station. Experience with all this was ideally suited to a boy who would grow up to fill a vital and much publicised role in public life.

The school also, inadvertently, introduced Charles to the less desirable side of being a public figure. Somehow the newspapers got to hear that Charles had been caught drinking alcohol while aged under 18. In itself the incident was not particularly important. Many teenagers have experimented with the odd tipple, though most do not indulge in highclass cherry brandy as did Prince Charles. It was the media attention it drew which was crucial. It showed that the press was still very much interested in the career of the heir. It also revealed to Prince Charles the importance of discretion for a man in his position.

His time at Gordonstoun culminated in a 6 month stay at Timbertop School at Geelong in Australia. Here, it is generally recognised, Charles lost the last of his boyish shyness and became fully prepared for the life ahead of him. After leaving Gordonstoun, Charles went up to Trinity College, Cambridge, where many important traits in his character emerged.

First, however, came his formal investiture as Prince of Wales. The ceremony itself was largely a form of medieval ritual recreated for the previous Prince of Wales as the actual medieval format had fallen into disuse centuries earlier. The investiture took place at Caernavon Castle, where the first Prince of Wales had been shown to his people in 1284. Charles was dressed in a cloak of purple velvet richly embroidered with gold and lined with ermine. The crown of Wales was placed on his head and the sceptre and sword placed in his hands. He then swore allegiance to the Queen to show that he held Wales on her behalf. The Queen and Prince then strode to a platform where he was formally introduced to the people of Wales. The tour of Wales which followed was Charles's first lengthy experience of public office, and the last for some time. As soon as the tour was over he returned to Cambridge.

At Cambridge Charles began to show a liking for music and acting. He practised both cello-playing and comedy acting enthusiastically for some time. The Goons, and goonish humour, were particularly appealing and Prince Charles became possibly the best-known fan of the offbeat comedy team. Unfortunately he was later forced to give up both the stage and music as the burden of his duties became increasingly heavy.

By the time he left university in 1970 Prince Charles had taken his seat in the House of Lords as Duke of Cornwall and had taken part in official visits to 8 nations, including Fiji, Australia and Canada. He then joined the services, in royal tradition, entering RAF Cranwell as an officer cadet. He stayed in the RAF for a year, long enough to add service wings to his private pilot's licence, before transferring to the navy.

In the navy, a service much favoured by royals, Prince Charles served in a variety of capacities before being given his own command in the shape of the minesweeper HMS *Bronington* in 1975. As captain of his ship Charles was expected to look after both the vessel and his men. It was a task many men of his age would have found daunting enough in itself, but Charles also had the added pressure of public life. In November 1976 the press was allowed on board HMS *Bronington* to film the prince commanding his vessel in a naval exercise in the Firth of Forth. The episode passed off without undue incident and journalists were able to report that the prince was a competent and respected officer.

Soon afterwards Prince Charles gave up the navy, though he retains honorary commissions in all three services, in order to concentrate more fully on his duties as a royal prince and heir to the throne. He embarked on a large number of tours, both within Britain and abroad. Two of the more highly publicised were the 1978 trip to Brazil, where he took part in the Rio Carnival with gusto and the visit to India for a meeting with Mother Teresa and a host of other engagements in 1980.

Of perhaps more interest are the causes and projects to which Prince Charles has given his support over the years. Not only have these provided the press with wonderful photo-opportunities and with some controversy, they have also given insights into the prince's character. After leaving the navy, Charles was prominent in fund-raising efforts for the British Trans-Globe Expedition which lived up to its name by setting off on a 35,000 mile journey around the world in the autumn of 1979. Soon afterwards the prince contributed his old cello and proceeds from his children's book *The Old Man of Lochnagar* to the appeal for the Royal Opera House, Covent Garden.

More engaging of his enthusiasm was the raising of the *Mary Rose*. The Tudor battleship had been built in around 1512 for Charles's ancestor King Henry VIII as the most modern warship afloat. After taking part in several successful actions she sank in 1545 when sailing out of Portsmouth hoping to pounce on a passing French fleet. The wreck settled deep in the Solent mud and was discovered by divers in 1968.

Ten years later a project to raise the wreck and place it on display were drawn up. Charles took an enthusiastic interest in the project, diving on the wreck no less than ten times. In October 1982 the ship had been fully prepared for lifting and Charles travelled to Portsmouth to be present. Continual technical problems cropped up to delay the event, and Charles stayed with friends. 'We've got to get her up' he declared to waiting journalists. Asked if this was a likely event the team leader, Peter Chittey, replied 'When a Prince tells you to get the ship up, you get it up'. They got it up.

The prince's attitude towards medicine has been rather more controversial. He is known to have an interest in homoeopathy and has made what were thought to be slightly veiled attacks on the medical establishment for supposedly not treating the patient as a whole human being, but merely attempting to cure the organ affected by disease.

But the most recent, most outspoken and most controversial of Prince Charles's opinions concern architecture. His interest in building design and concept goes back many years, but the first warning shot did not come until 1984. In that year the Prince was invited to speak to the Royal Institute of British Architects. In the course of his speech he denounced a proposed extension to the National Gallery as 'a monstrous carbuncle on the face of a much-loved and elegant friend'.

The broadside of royal disfavour was delivered in 1988 in a 75 minute documentary film written by Prince Charles and shown on the BBC. In the film the Prince comprehensively castigated the modernist architects with their insistence on designing bare expanses of concrete and large scale and high-rise developments. Prince Charles spoke passionately in favour of more human scale planning and a greater focus on attractiveness and detail. The architects largely slammed his comments as being reactionary or even wrong. The public, however, supported him with overwhelming fervour. In the architectural episode, Prince Charles undoubtedly trod on a lot of important toes, but he also summed up the feelings of the silent majority.

Through the 1970s Prince Charles was gradually filling out his role as heir to the throne, but one aspect of his life remained unsettled, that of his marriage. Whoever the dashing young prince decided to marry could expect to become Queen in due course. His choice of bride was, therefore, of prime importance not only to himself but also to the nation and the Common-wealth.

For the young lady concerned the acceptance of the proposal would mean far more than a normal decision to marry. She would not only be taking on a husband and a new role as a married woman, but would also be stepping into the full glare of public attention. Stability of personality and a love of family life were paramount requirements as were discretion and tact. Clearly it was not so much a marriage as a career. King George VI referred to the royal family as 'The Firm', and in many ways it is run along business lines. Recruiting a new member of staff through marriage was going to be a tough task for Prince Charles.

All these considerations influenced royal watchers to advocate two distinct courses. One school of thinking felt that it would be most sensible for Prince Charles to choose a member of a foreign royal family. Such a lady would already be accustomed to the pressures and duties of a royal lifestyle and so would slip into the role of Princess of Wales with the minimum of fuss and difficulty.

A second group of royal watchers predicted that the Prince would opt to marry a daughter of one of the premier noble houses of Britain. They argued that there were simply not enough eligible royal princesses to choose from with the number of royal families around the world rapidly dwindling. They were also confident that such a match would be popular in Britain and that it was more in keeping with the more relaxed style of monarchy in the late 20th century.

Only a few eccentrics predicted that Charles might follow

the disastrous lead of his great-uncle, King Edward VIII, and marry for love.

The years after Prince Charles left the navy kept the royal watchers and gossip columnists busy. A succession of likely candidates for Princess of Wales appeared on the scene. Most of them faded away without a hint of romance, except in the press. There were others who appeared to be more serious contenders.

The favourite choice among those who felt Charles would marry royalty was Princess Marie-Astrid of Luxembourg, the elder daughter of the Grand Duke. Not only was the lady of a suitable age, she was also very obviously regal. Unfortunately she was also a Roman Catholic and therefore barred by law from becoming Princess of Wales. Such a fact only served to suggest in some quarters that a constitutional crisis was imminent. Princess Caroline of Monaco was also, briefly, linked to Prince Charles in the newspapers. Charles himself dismissed the reports by stating 'I have only met the girl once'. Not even those who favoured an arranged royal match believed Charles could marry someone he knew so slightly.

When the Prince of Wales eventually announced his choice it caught nearly everyone by surprise. The eccentrics had been proved right and Charles married for love. His choice was Lady Diana Spencer, younger daughter of Earl Spencer. The Spencers first gained prominence in the days of the Tudors and gained their earldom towards the end of the 17th century. Lady Diana was the younger of three daughters of the 8th Duke and was born in 1961 to a family which was landed, but not overwhelmingly wealthy. Much of the family treasure had to be sold off to maintain the estate during Diana's teenage years.

It is likely that Lady Diana first met Prince Charles in 1977 when he was briefly dating her elder sister Sarah, but romance did not blossom until the spring of 1980. Diana was a guest at Balmoral in the summer when the shared interest in salmon fishing brought her and Prince Charles together. Somehow the national press got wind of the fact that Prince Charles had acquired a girlfriend. When Lady Diana returned to London to continue with her job as a kindergarten teacher it was to find herself a celebrity. Any chance of a private life was over.

Though the reporters continued to dog Diana's footsteps they found out little. Private meetings with the Prince of Wales were arranged. Usually the reporters were thrown off the track either by one of Diana's three flatmates or by adroit driving through London's busy streets. The couple were, however, seen out together at race meetings and at parties. Sometimes the press speculation or reporting became rather too intense and drew admonishments from the Palace or from Diana's mother.

An official tour of India by Charles in November was intensively covered with the reporters asking constant questions about the romance. All they could draw from the taciturn prince was the admission 'I'm terrified of getting it wrong'. In the circumstances it was an understandable reaction. Charles must have known what a trying time Lady Diana was having at the hands of the press.

Finally, on 4th February Charles proposed over dinner at Buckingham Palace and was at once accepted. It is said that Charles wanted to give Diana and her family time to think things over. He knew better than anyone the pressures of the new life Diana would lead. The official announcement was therefore put off until the 24th. In the event there was no change of heart and the date of the wedding was set for 29th July.

At once the 19 year old Lady Diana became a royal in waiting and was launched into the full glare of publicity. She moved to Clarence House to stay with the Queen Mother for the months leading up to the wedding and abandoned forever what remained of her private life. To the newspapers she was already 'Lady Di', but now her official title after the wedding became a thorny subject. Officially she would become 'Diana, Princess of Wales' or would take her husband's name as 'Princess Charles of Wales'. Perhaps inevitably the tabloids decided to use the more informal, and incorrect 'Princess Diana', and the term has become common usage.

But if the press were piling the pressure on Diana, she was not one to take it meekly. She struck back in daring and novel fashion. Several commentators had already noticed that Lady Diana's tall slim figure was outstandingly elegant and well suited to wearing clothes. Some even described her as well-proportioned enough to be a model.

At the official engagement photocall Diana allowed her outfit to take second place to her engagement ring. The ring was a magnificent creation of a large sapphire surrounded by a cluster of diamonds. Its cost was not revealed by experts estimated that it had probably drawn a price tag of around £28,000. Nevertheless her dark blue suit with its reverse pleated skirt and open jacket gathered at the waist over a high-necked blouse set off by a neck bow drew some comment. More careful fashion commentators predicted that the new royal would prove to be a trend-setter. Others feared that her youth and inexperience might lead to embarrassments. Nobody was prepared for the triumphs of fashion with which Lady Diana stunned the world.

On 3rd March she accompanied Prince Charles to a film premiere. When she stepped from the official car her outfit drew gasps from the many who had gathered to see her. She emerged in a vibrant full length evening gown of glaring flame red decorated with applied gold designs. The low neckline showed off a magnificent gold and cornelian necklace.

Impressive as the red dress was, it was as nothing compared to the creation Diana sported six days later when she attended a music recital at Goldsmith's Hall, London. She appeared in a black silk taffeta evening dress with a full skirt. The matching shawl with an ornate fringe covered a daringly low boned strapless bodice which threatened to reveal more than fashion demanded and etiquette allowed with almost every move made. It was, however, cunningly tailored to remain in place and was charmingly set off by a diamond necklace and earrings. Diana's next official appearance was looked forward to with eagerness by fashion editors and ladies everywhere.

The event came on 25th March when Diana visited Sandown Races in Surrey. She wore a highly conventional, but no less appealing, brown two piece suit. Though far from innovative, the outfit was ideally suited to the occasion. Clearly the new member of the royal family was one whom fashion writers would have to watch carefully.

Over the following months the chief subject of conversation in the fashion world was the wedding dress. It soon became known that Lady Diana had approached the Emmanuels to design the gown. The dress-designer couple were well-known for producing exciting new variations on traditional themes. It was confidently expected they would produce a suitable dress. Reporters, of course, fired a barrage of questions when ever the designers appeared in the hope of eliciting some titbit of news about the wedding gown. There was even talk of journalists grubbing through refuse bins to try to find offcuts and so discover the chosen material.

All the speculation came to an end when Lady Diana stepped from her carriage to ascend the steps of St Paul's Cathedral. In its way the wedding dress was every bit as spectacular as had been the strapless black evening gown which had launched Diana on to the fashion stage. Everyone had been talking about a fairytale wedding, and Diana provided them with a fairytale wedding dress.

The basic dress was of ivory silk taffeta cut into a shaped bodice with deep V neckline and a full puffball skirt. The bodice was overlaid with embroidered lace and patterned with intricate designs of mother of pearl and sequins. The low neckline was embellished with richly rouched silk and a large bow. The sleeves were puffed at the shoulders and gathered at the elbow. The train was in matching silk with hand-embroidered lace fringes. The gossamer silk veil was topped off by the Spencer family tiara which was appropriately of an entwined heart design.

The wedding itself was a magnificent display not only of the pomp and regality of royalty but also of patriotism. The streets of London were thronged with hundreds of thousands of well wishers. As on so many other great royal occasions, the gutters along the route were soon awash with corks, bottle-tops and food scraps as the crowds celebrated in their own way.

At the cathedral the marriage service continued. The 17th century building was packed with foreign dignitaries, lords and ladies. It also contained television crews who took pictures transmitted live to an estimated world-wide audience of 750 million people. The crowds outside listened eagerly to every word transmitted to them. When the final vows were exchanged the solemn silence within the cathedral was interrupted by ecstatic cheers drifting in from outside.

After the wedding breakfast Diana and Charles left Buckingham Palace for their honeymoon. Once again Diana scored a fashion triumph with an outfit of cantaloupe-coloured silk and matching bolero jacket. The honeymoon itself sparked something of an international incident when the royal couple flew to Gibraltar to board the Royal Yacht *Britannia* for a Mediterranean cruise. Spain, which claims Gibralter, protested at the move.

Since that wedding day, Diana has more than fulfilled her early promise as a trend-setter in the world of fashion. Her every outfit has been closely studied by fashion writers and fashion designers over the years. Clothes shops wishing to capture the young end of the clothes market have been well advised to reflect the taste of the Princess of Wales in their stock. Each major royal tour or event has been a time of intense interest for fashion houses around the world. What would the Princess of Wales be wearing?

But it is not only as a arbiter of fashion that the Princess of Wales has made the headlines. Within only four months of the wedding it was announced that she was expecting her first child. Immediately press speculation about morning sickness and other problems became intense. In the event there were few, if any, medical problems associated with the pregnancy. Most intense was speculation as to whether the birth would take place at the palace, as tradition demanded, or in hospital. Not until the princess arrived at St Mary's Hospital in the early morning of 21st June was the question resolved. Even then the press missed the arrival. There was not a single reporter or photographer on duty at the time.

At eleven o'clock that evening Prince Charles left the hospital announcing that his new son was both beautiful and marvellous. Another break with royal convention came when mother and child appeared in front of the press the day after the birth, rather than waiting a longer period of time. The chosen names were announced a week later as William Arthur Philip Louis and the child was christened six weeks later.

Thereafter the young prince almost vanished from public view until a surprise photocall just before Christmas. Prince William romped happily around a sofa while his parents answered a continuous stream of questions from attendant journalists. But one fact was clear without a single question needing to be asked. The young prince was a descendant of the Spencers. There was already more than enough individual character in the face to show a strong resemblance to his maternal grandfather, Earl Spencer who himself shows strong a family likeness to his forebears.

In March of the following year the Wales couple surprised nearly everyone by breaking with royal tradition and taking Prince William with them on an extended tour of Australia and New Zealand. The youngster spent most of his time on a ranch while his parents toured various areas. The Princess of Wales, however, ensured that she was allowed plenty of days off from official duties so that she could return to her baby.

Over the following years, Prince William has progressed through the usual stages of toddling, climbing into wastepaper baskets and going to primary school. In 1984 he was joined by a brother, Prince Henry Charles Albert David who quickly proved to be as popular with the public as had Prince William. The cheerful and popular Earl Spencer greeted the news of a new grandson with the hope that he would 'one day play cricket for Gloucestershire'. It was, perhaps, the hope of a great many Gloucestermen for not only is the royal couple's home in Gloucestershire, but Henry was the name of the late Duke of Gloucester.

The arrival of two new, glamorous and popular royal ladies through the medium of lavish wedding celebrations and the equally rapid appearance of four new royal children has tended to push the more established royals somewhat into the background of the publicity glare. For the most part they have accepted the change gracefully. Indeed, they may almost have welcomed it as an opportunity to get on with their duties and private lives without the constant intrusion of a mob of journalists and photographers.

Princess Anne is a case in point. When she was born in 1950 she was third in the line to the throne. When her mother succeeded to the throne two years later, Anne was raised to second in line to the throne after her elder brother Charles. By the age of 14 she had been relegated to fourth in line after the birth of two younger brothers. During her early years her childhood had been covered in detail by the press, which continued to take an interest in the only unmarried British princess.

The Princess has always been known as a blunt and straightforward person. In many ways this has come as a useful contrast to the continuous good manners and tact of other royals, but it has also involved Princess Anne in not a little controversy over the years. When journalists have become too intrusive or persistent, particularly at non-official events, Princess Anne has often told them exactly where to go in no uncertain terms. The encounter has then been widely reported, usually with little reference to the pressure which prompted the outburst.

Despite these unfortunate little storms, Princess Anne gained much popularity during the early 1970s. Her first official function without the support of her family came in 1968. Within a very few months it became clear that Anne was embracing the latest fashions and styles with gusto. She appeared in a succession of trouser suits, mini-skirts and low-heeled shoes in a dazzling display of bright, almost vivid colours. So sudden and complete was her coming out that Princess Anne was sometimes accused of trying to upstage the Queen. The newspapers called her the 'Swinging Princess'. Anne managed to tone down such talk effectively.

Before long her interest in horses had become well known, as had her considerable skill in equestrian sports. In 1971 her dazzling horsemanship won her the European Championship and it was confidently expected that the string of minor trophies would continue to pile up.

In the equestrian world Princess Anne met a variety of good-looking and eligible young men. Though the press paid some attention to her marriage prospects, the openness of her friendships indicated that they were that and nothing more. It was therefore not surprising that when she began to be seen in the company of a certain Lieutenant Mark Phillips, a member of the 1972 Olympic Team, few took the relationship very seriously. Not until 1973 did the royal watchers consider that there might be anything romantic in the association. The couple became engaged in May and married within six months.

After the wedding came the sensational attempt to kidnap Princess Anne in 1974. The attack was only foiled when the Princess's personal detective pounced on a gunman who was trying to drag Princess Anne from her car in The Mall. Two years later Princess Anne competed in the 1976 Olympics as part of the British Equestrian Team, but failed to win a medal.

Thereafter Princess Anne gradually slipped out of the public limelight as she spent increasing amounts of time on her duties and family life. The only large scale publicity which surrounded her concerned her growing children and periodic rumours of domestic strife.

All that changed in 1984 when Princess Anne undertook an arduous tour in her capacity as patron of the Save the Children Fund. From the first it was obvious to even the most disinterested observer that this tour was distinctly unusual. Before she left Britain, Princess Anne made it clear to Save the Children Fund officials that she wanted to see what was really happening, not a sanitised view considered fit for delicate royal sensibilities. She got what she wanted.

The tour of eight nations in Africa and the Middle East was long, arduous and harrowing. It was also dangerous. The areas due to be visited were amongst the most disease-ridden on Earth so Princess Anne had to endure an impressively long list of inoculations before leaving home.

There was also the more immediate risk of violent death. Many of the places to be visited were in war zones or were subject to the rule of highly suspicious and trigger-happy regimes. As if to prove this the members of the advance party arriving in Zimbabwe were arrested at gunpoint on vague suspicion of espionage and were only released after intense diplomatic pressure.

A journey to refugee camps in Somalia was cancelled at the last minute when the Ogaden War, which the refugees were fleeing, spilled over the border uncomfortably close to the camps. When the fighting eased, the Princess insisted on visiting the tent city housing 40,000 people she had been due to tour. There she found all too much evidence of the human misery caused by wars, together with disease and overworked doctors.

When visiting the Victoria Falls Princess Anne was accompanied by a large armed guard because of an outbreak of tribal warfare in Matabeleland. But the most perilous leg of her tour was undoubtedly the visit to Beirut. Only a few days earlier a bomb blast had killed over 50 people and the vicious civil war raged unchecked. Undaunted the Princess stayed in the shattered city for a full day, meeting the beleaguered President Gemayel and visiting refugee camps.

The tour brought Princess Anne an immediate rush of public support. For the first time her enormous workload for deserving causes was perceived by the people at large. The year following the Save the Children Fund tour Princess Anne was inundated with more invitations than usual and did her best to attend as many as she could. Everything from visiting the Wolverston housing scheme for the elderly to attending the Young Farmers Club Annual General Meeting came to Princess Anne.

It was unfortunate that the increase in public popularity and profile for Princess Anne should be so quickly followed by renewed gossip about the state of her marriage. It was noticed that Captain Mark Phillips was spending rather more time managing his estates at Gatcombe than on accompanying his wife on official tours. Captain Phillips's entirely reasonable retort that he was not on the Civil List and therefore was under no obligation to attend official duties, and also had to earn a living, stilled speculation for a while.

Rumours came again in 1988 and eventually it was announced that the couple had decided to separate. There was no suggestion of a divorce, however, and the couple appeared to remain on friendly terms. There was, at least, little sign of the kind of acrimonious disputes which mark some separations.

Also liable to rather uneven press coverage and public approval is Prince Edward, the youngest of the Queen's children. Born in 1964 Prince Edward's progression through childhood has always been rather overshadowed by the exploits of the older members of the royal family. By the time Edward was sent to Gordonstoun his two elder brothers had also passed through that establishment's doors and the idea of a royal prince attending school was rather too old hat for newspapers to remark upon.

What did become clear at Gordonstoun was that Prince Edward was the most academically gifted of the Queen's children. His studies were much more highly praised than had been those of his brothers and it was confidently predicted he would go on to university. First, however, Prince Edward travelled to New Zealand to spend a year as a trainee teacher at Wanganui Collegiate, just outside the capital Wellington.

The post he took up was no sinecure. It involved not only teaching potentially unruly schoolboys English grammar and literature, but also the whole range of school activities. Prince Edward was expected to lead groups on long hikes, sometimes staying overnight in the wilder regions of New Zealand. On one trip he had the unenviable task of keeping a camp full of boys entertained and out of mischief for an evening.

While in New Zealand, Prince Edward was largely separated from the round of royal engagements being undertaken by his family, but not from the attention of the press. Several newspapers both from New Zealand and Britain sent photographers to Wanganui in the hope of catching a newsworthy photograph of the Prince. On the whole they failed to discover anything except that Prince Edward did not enjoy having his duties interrupted by unwanted intrusions. He told the reporters what he felt and, as with some of Princess Anne's remarks, his comments were reported in the press.

Prince Edward did find respite from the reporters on his eight day trip to Antarctica. There he not only visited the South Pole, but also was shown huts used by Captain Scott on his ill-fated effort to be the first human at the South Pole. After paying visits to the various scientific stations on the frozen continent, Prince Edward returned to Wanganui.

In May he returned to England after declaring that 'I'm not cut out to be a teacher'. Instead he underwent a two week training stint with the Royal Marines at Lympstone in order to be counted as a cadet before going up to Cambridge. Despite being less robustly outgoing than his two elder brothers, and the fact that one marine officer described the course as 'Hell', Prince Edward passed with flying colours.

Prince Edward went up in October amid a storm of controversy. His examination results were leaked to the press and proved to be not as good as expected. There was a suspicion that Prince Edward had been accepted by Jesus College on account of his royalty rather than his qualifications and there was ugly talk of fellow students ostracising him. The Master of the College, however, insisted that Prince Edward had, like other students, been accepted on the basis of headmaster's report, personal interview and examination results. The fact that nine other students had been offered places on A-level results lower than those of Prince Edward served to still the murmurs of criticism.

At Cambridge Prince Edward read archaeology and anthropology and gradually slipped out of the press limelight, though the occasional incident did make its way into national newspapers. When Prince Edward and his personal detective were photographed illegally riding their bicycles along the pavement, there was a flurry of interest. More interest was caused by his participation in the college's rugby team. In Prince Edward's first game for the college, the team was thrashed by a margin of 23 points. A victory of 18-4 at the next outing increased his respectability as a player.

Most media interest, however, revolved around a game against St John's College. Prince Edward spotted a loose ball and raced for it, diving to the ground in an effort to beat a burly opposition player scooping the ball. Prince Edward failed, instead receiving a heavy blow on the head as he collided with his opponent. The prince was concussed and was carried away on a stretcher to receive medical attention. The injury failed to dampen Prince Edward's ardour for the game and he continued to play for his college.

Of perhaps rather more relevance to the future than either his rugby or archaeology was Prince Edward's involvement with undergraduate drama. Almost as soon as he arrived at Cambridge, Prince Edward joined the Jesus College Drama Society. His attempt to gain a part in the autumn play *The Crucible* was successful. He landed the opportunity to play the judge Danforth who presided over the terrible Salem witch-hunts of the 17th century. It was a demanding role, calling for passion and fear to be expressed through the set speeches. The critics agreed that Prince Edward played his part well. And it was clear to all present that he greatly enjoyed the opportunity to show his acting skills.

Soon afterwards he joined the team producing *The Glitter Ball Prizes*, the university rag week revue. Prince Edward did not appear on stage this time, but was heavily involved with behind the scenes work. The most visible activity in which he participated was a publicity stunt to drum up interest in the show. He acted as driver of a taxi on top of which was a wooden board carrying two fellow undergraduates busily dancing to taped music. Whether this slightly offbeat attempt was responsible or not, the show was sold out several days before the performance and raised over £500 for charity.

On leaving university with a respectable, though not brilliant, degree Prince Edward renewed his relationship with the Royal Marines by enrolling in the officer training course. It appeared that Prince Edward was set on following his two elder brothers into a service life, though whether he would turn it into a career, as Prince Andrew has done, was unclear.

In the event Prince Edward did not complete the arduous course. Like many other hopefuls, Prince Edward decided that the Royal Marines, like teaching, was not for him. He resigned from the Marines and took up a post in the Really Useful Theatre Company, a theatrical production team run by Andrew Lloyd-Webber. Charged with running the hugely successful West End musicals written by Lloyd-Webber, the Really Useful Theatre Company is both busy and exciting. No doubt Prince Edward is finding a suitable outlet for his theatrical talents in this new career.

Watching the progress of their four children through childhood to adulthood and new found public profile are their parents, the Queen and Prince Philip. Unlike all other members of the royal family, the Queen has an important role within the constitution of Great Britain. Indeed it is this complex and vital role which provides the reason why the royal family continues to be of such importance to Britain.

Yet the role of the monarch in the constitution is remarkably unclear and ill defined. Britain is one of the few nations on earth not to have a written constitution in which the powers and rights of various individuals and bodies are set out. In theory the Queen rules the nation with the advice of her ministers. It is she who makes laws, declares war or arranges treaties. In practice it is the democratically elected House of Commons and the House of Lords which perform all the duties of government. Their respective powers and duties are set out in a complex mass of documents and laws dating back many centuries. Much of British government is run on tradition which has no legal validity at all, except that of usage.

The monarch's role in government is equally obscure. It is perhaps best summed up by the famous declaration of Bagehot that the monarch has 'the right to be consulted, the right to encourage and the right to warn'. The Queen has frequent and regular meetings with the Prime Minister of the day to discuss current events and government policy.

Occasionally more obvious indications of the monarch's power are seen. In 1957 the Queen was faced with having to name a new Prime Minister when there was no obvious candidate. Usually the Queen chooses the leader of the majority party in the House of Commons, but in 1957 the Conservative Party was in a majority and without a leader. The Queen consulted with the senior figures in the Conservative Party and with courtiers, and chose Harold Macmillan as the man best able to lead the government. It is now unlikely that such a situation would repeat itself for today all political parties have set procedures for choosing their own leaders.

In 1975 Australia provided another instance in which the royal prerogative was called upon to settle a political problem. In that year the two houses of parliament became caught in hopeless deadlock. Sir John Kerr, Governor General of Australia, stepped in to sort out the difficulty. Using his powers as the representative of the Queen in Australia, he dismissed Prime Minister Gough Whitlam and installed the more liberal Malcolm Fraser to lead the government until a general election could be held. Politicians and constitutional lawyers were astounded by the move, but it merely reflected the power of the monarch to bypass the politicians in an emergency.

More usually the Queen's role in government is less direct. As the only head of state of a major nation to have remained in position for approaching 40 years she has a wealth of experience and knowledge to draw upon. This is most noticeable in foreign affairs, particularly when dealing with the Commonwealth. In 1979 a conference of Commonwealth leaders was held in Lusaka which both the Queen and the newly elected Prime Minister Margaret Thatcher attended. The help the Queen was able to offer her chief minister in introductions to various foreign dignitaries was noticeable and effective.

The Queen also helped calm a potentially embarrassing event when the Mayor of Lusaka made what was supposed to be a speech of welcome. Instead he took the opportunity to blaze at his political opponents and fire some well-aimed shots at foreign powers. He then asked the Queen to reply. 'No thank you' she said with a firmness and icy tone which effectively stopped the ceremony in its tracks.

Also in the field of foreign affairs are the state visits paid to Britain each year, or which the Queen pays to other nations. Generally speaking there are two major state visits to Britain each year, though heads of state of less important nations provide additional guests. In 1983 the President of France was followed to London within a week by the King of Tonga. The Queen's involvement in state visits is formalized and standard. She entertains the visitor to a state banquet at Buckingham Palace, Windsor Castle or Holyrood House and then attends the banquet hosted by the visitor at a major hotel. Thereafter the Queen's role is rather limited, unless the guest is a particular acquaintance.

More usually the Queen's schedule revolves around routine formal events. She receives visits from various diplomats, either British or foreign, and invests honours and medals on those deserving individuals recommended to her. There are, in addition, the endless number of public engagements which are attended, be they a regimental dinner, the opening of new hospital ward or a tour of a new museum or gallery. It is at these events that the Queen is most in the public eye, though they are arguably the least important part of her duties. It is at the public engagements that the Queen shows her taste in clothes, her tact and charm to the largest audience. With the advent of television the audience may be several million strong. It is to her great credit that such events usually pass off without a hitch.

The Queen has had a long and exhaustive career in public service to prepare her for the work she does today. Unlike Prince Charles, she was not considered destined for the throne from birth. When she was born in 1926, Princess Elizabeth was the daughter of a younger son of King George V. It was confidentlyl expected that her uncle, Edward Prince of Wales, would inherit the throne. The future birth of a younger borther would also of stopped Princess Elizabeth inheriting her father's claim to the throne.

The Queen has had a long and exhaustive career in public service to prepare her for the work she does today. Unlike Prince Charles, she was not considered destined for the throne from birth. When she was born in 1926, Princess Elizabeth was the daughter of a younger son of King George V. It was confidently expected that her uncle, Edward Prince of Wales, would inherit the throne. The future birth of a younger brother would also have stopped Princess Elizabeth inheriting her father's claim to the throne.

In the event Princess Elizabeth's uncle had been on the throne only a matter of months as Edward VIII when he abdicated in order to marry Wallis Simpson, a twice divorced American woman whom most people considered unsuitable to be a queen. Suddenly ten-year-old Princess Elizabeth was heir to the throne. She was plunged into the training and grooming necessary for a future monarch at once. She learnt well so that when she began taking her father's place at state functions in 1951, due to his ill health, she acted with perfect tact and decorum. The death of George VI in 1952 put Princess Elizabeth on the throne as Queen Elizabeth II. The nation hailed the occasion as the start of a new Elizabethan age of grandeur and hope such as had existed under the great Elizabeth I. The euphoria lasted some time, but has now settled down into a genuine appreciation of the work which the Queen does as sovereign.

The Queen's consort, Prince Philip, has a position even more ambiguous than that of his wife. Unlike the wife of a king he has no title gained by marriage. His royal rank derives from his descent from the Greek royal family while his title of Duke of Edinburgh was conferred on him by King George VI. He was born in Corfu in 1921 and at the age of 18 months was packed off to Switzerland in a converted orange box while his father narrowly escaped execution consequent on a revolution. Thereafter the Greek royal family lived in exile, with Prince Philip being brought up in Britain.

He joined the Royal Navy as World War II was breaking out and rose rapidly to become a lieutenant at the age of just 21. In 1942 he faced enemy fire at the Battle of Cape Mattapan, as his son would do off the Falklands forty years later, and was mentioned in despatches. After the war he gained his first command, the frigate HMS *Magpie*. Meanwhile, he had met Princess Elizabeth who was five years young than himself. During the war years the friendship deepened into love and the engagement was announced in July 1947 with the wedding taking place four months later. Prince Philip continued with his naval duties for some time, but in 1951 increasing number of public engagements forced him to take extended leave. He never returned to the navy, but he has not left either and is still technically on leave.

Prince Philip soon found that it was not easy being a consort. He had no constitutional position and no set duties. Instead he decided to set his own agenda and list of activities. Often his well-intentioned efforts to become involved were regarded as busy-body interfering while activities the promotoers of which lobbied for his attention were not always those he felt he wanted to attend. He has, however, managed to find his own way. Paying careful deference to his wife's precedence when in public has ensured he does not steal her limelight while his friendly manner and easy style ensure that many people meet a member of the royal family while the Queen concentrates on the business in hand.

When on his own Prince Philip plays a variety of roles. On foreign visits, as many as 25 a year, he meets government figures and British residents. He is also patron, president or has links with organisations as diverse as the Royal Ocean Racing Club, World Wildlife Fund and Duke of Edinburgh's Award Scheme. Most controversial among his many activities is his love of shooting and hunting. This has drawn periodic press comment, particularly when contrasted with his work for conservation organisations.

As Prince Philip himself has explained on a number of occasions his concern for the wildlife of the world revolves around the preservation of species and ecosystems, not the welfare of individual animals. Indeed the pheasants, grouse and deer which Prince Philip pursues in his leisure time are bred and reared specially for the sport. There is no more environmental damage caused by properly organised hunting than in the slaughter of bacon pigs. Indeed, it could be argued that hunting can be an environmentally friendly exercise in that it preserves large areas of land from development.

Another area of controversy which has surrounded the Duke of Edinburgh on occasion is that of off-the-cuff remarks. The informal and easy style which the prince has adopted leads to his making throw-away remarks to bystanders which the press delight in taking out of context and blowing up into major faux pas. For the most part the remarks have been harmless enough in intent and meaning, but were vulnerable to considerable misinterpretation.

Of perhaps more interest is the way the Duke of Edinburgh will make controversial speeches which unashamedly take sides in an argument. His call in 1980 against a boycott of the Moscow Olympics was a plea for sportsmanship but was widely interpreted as a snub to America, which called for the ban, and for Mrs Thatcher who supported it. He has even waded into the treacherous waters of nuclear debate, declaring that the point at issue 'is not the nuclear weapons, but the scruples of their possessors'. It was a remark which could be applied to any weapon with equal truth, but was not designed to endear him to anti-nuclear protestors.

In spite of, or perhaps because of, his individualistic approach to his royal status, Prince Philip has become one of the most respected royals. His work for projects which have gained his attention is tireless, while he has not allowed royal protocol to mask his personal opinions entirely. Many people suspect that the fervent involvement of Prince Charles in so many crusades, such as that against modernist architecture, is due to the influence of the Duke of Edinburgh. The Duke's children have all paid tribute to him and it is not unreasonable to assume that they have all benefited greatly from having the Duke as a father.

The Queen's younger sister, Princess Margaret, receives rather less press coverage than the other members of the Queen's immediate family. In part this may be due to the fact that she is not perceived as being a favourite royal with the public, but it is certainly no reflection on the number or scope of her public work. The list of official engagements of Princess Margaret is as long as that of many others on the civil list and includes the usual diverse range from horticultural shows to charity lunches or gala performances.

Indeed there is a strong artistic leaning in the official engagements of Princess Margaret which is not so obvious in those of other members of the royal family. It reflects the fact that of all her relatives, Princess Margaret is the one most interested in and most knowledgable about the arts. She attends numerous plays and operas, both as official engagements and privately and is an inveterate party-goer. Many of these parties are well attended by show business stars and personalities.

Like Prince Edward, Princess Margaret is not content to enjoy the talents of others, but will also perform herself. Unlike her nephew, however, Princess Margaret has not walked the boards. Instead she entertains at parties and before her house guests. Those who have witnessed such performances usually praise her gifts as an impersonater, show business figures being among those she likes to mimic.

The present round of partying and official functions is the result of a career in public service which has not always been of the happiest. As a child Princess Margaret was feted wherever she went and pursued by the press. For many years she was second in line to the throne, a position she was not to lose until her elder sister gave birth to Prince Charles in 1948.

During the bleak war years Princess Margaret joined her elder sister in morale-boosting work. They were photographed knitting socks for soldiers, made radio broadcasts to the children of the nation and made numerous public appearances to show the public that the royal family was staying put. King George VI was determined that his people would never think the royal family would flee abroad as so many Continental dynasties had done.

Immediately after the war Princess Margaret saw her elder sister fall in love and marry. It was widely thought that Princess Margaret's turn would not be long in arriving. By the time Coronation Year came about rumours were beginning to circulate that the 23-year-old princess had fallen in love with a member of the Royal Household, Group Captain Peter Townsend the former royal equerry to King George VI. At first the public was uncertain as to the truth of the talk. When Group Captain Townsend was retained as equerry to the new Queen, and was seen chatting amiably with members of the royal family it was generally assumed that the supposed romance had merely been a friendship. Some hint of gossip, however, continued to surface from time to time.

When the news of the romance did break in earnest in 1955, it caused a sensation. There were distant echoes of the Abdication Crisis of just seventeen years earlier for Group Captain Townsend, like Wallis Simpson, was divorced. In itself this caused enormous problems for the royal family. As head of the Church of England and a person held up as a moral model for the nation, the Queen was painfully aware that the church did not recognise divorce. Christian law declared that Group Captain Townsend was still married and that any ceremony undertaken with Princess Margaret would be bigamous.

For week after week the affair dragged on in the press. The official palace spokesmen refused to be drawn on the question of the romance and speculation ran amok. The eventual outcome was almost inevitable. The Queen had to persuade her sister to issue a statement declaring that she would not marry Group Captain Townsend 'being mindful of the Church's teaching that Christian marriage is indissoluble, and conscious of my duty towards the Commonwealth'.

Townsend slipped away from Court to glide into graceful obscurity and in time the affair died down. It had, however, caused much discussion among the public. Though opinions differed there was an overall feeling that shadowy, faceless people at 'Court' had perhaps too much influence over the royal family. There was much comment in the press, that the Court was restraining the royal family from moving with the times and was holding them back in the 19th century. It was talk which reappeared occasionally over the following years and did not vanish until much of the pomp of court life had been quietly abandoned and the royals became more dedicated to meeting ordinary people than previously.

The love life of Princess Margaret again leapt into public view in February 1960 when her engagement was announced to Antony Armstrong-Jones. The move astounded the public and came as a great surprise to the majority of gossip columnists who prided themselves on keeping abreast of royal events. At the time Antony Armstrong-Jones was working as a photographer. His list of clients included some imposing names, including those of the royal family, but his circle of friends was decidedly modern, almost bohemian.

Even more alarming for those who held the establishment notion of a sutiable groom was the fact that his father was twice divorced and that there was no title in his family. After the wedding Princess Margaret became known simply as Mrs Armstrong-Jones. Perhaps more than any other this enormously popular match helped break the aura of remoteness which had surrounded the royal family in the 1950s. The feeling was somewhat broken in 1961 when the Queen granted Antony Armstrong-Jones the title of Earl Snowdon. At the time of the investiture, Princess Margaret was pregnant with her first child. It was widely believed that either the Queen, Princess Margaret or both, had insisted on the title so that direct descendants of King George VI would have a noble rank of some kind.

The early years of the marriage passed in blissful happiness for the couple, but towards the end of the 1970s press speculation of a rift in the relationship began to gain in strength. Soon the couple announced their separation and a quiet divorce was arranged. Even then the press did not leave Princess Margaret alone, but continued to search for a basis of a fresh romance. They eventually found it in the shape of one Roddy Llewellyn, who was pursued relentlessly by reporters and photographers until any relationship which had existed came to an end.

The oldest member of the royal family, and possibly the most loved, is the Queen Mother who in 1990 celebrates her 90th birthday. Despite her great age, the Queen Mother has refused to be pushed into retirement either by the advice of doctors or by the advent of younger royals to take over her duties. It may be true that the two or three dozen engagements which she undertakes each year are rather more sedate and less demanding than those of her children and grandchildren, but it is wonderful that she is able to attend at all. There can be no doubt as to the genuine warmth of the reception she receives wherever she goes.

It is a warmth which has been evident ever since the then Lady Elizabeth Bowes-Lyon first entered public life nearly seventy years ago. Born on 4th August 1900 as the ninth of ten children of Lord Glamis, Lady Elizabeth spent a childhood typical of her class in the Edwardian era. The First World War turned her family home into a convalescent home for the injured, with Lady Elizabeth helping the staff, and cost the family five deaths.

Having been launched into society as a debutante, Lady Elizabeth became friends with Princess Mary and through her met Prince Albert, Duke of York and the future George VI. The shy young prince was immediately captivated by the graceful daughter of Lord Glamis and in 1922 he proposed. Lady Elizabeth turned him down, apparently because she was unwilling to take on everything which a royal lifestyle demanded. But a second proposal in January 1923 was successful and the wedding took place that April, making Lady Elizabeth the new Duchess of York.

It is curious that the Queen Mother should at first have been so reluctant to enter the royal family for from the moment the engagement was announced she has shown herself adept at the many duties and tasks demanded of her. King George V and his majestic wife Queen Mary were very taken with her, a fact which quickly became clear to the public. The press clamoured around the young couple just as they would around the children and grandchildren of the Queen Mother as their engagements were announced. 'The cat is out of the bag,' Lady Elizabeth wrote to a friend at about this time, 'and there is no way of stuffing him back in.'

The marriage worked well, with the new Duchess of York supporting her quiet and conscientious husband in all the work he had to undertake. When the Abdication Crisis loomed, the Yorks found themselves unwitting players. The Yorks did not meet King Edward VIII's love until after the death of George V. The Duchess of York disliked Wallis Simpson on sight. As the months passed the Duchess became increasingly appalled by the way the new king was ignoring his duties for his personal life. It would seem that she felt even more keenly the fact that she and her husband were kept in complete ignorance of what was happening by the king. Only a short time before the abdication were they given any hint that such an event was coming.

Suddenly and surprisingly the Duke of York was set upon the throne as King George VI. It was not a role which came naturally to a quiet, shy man like the new king. That he managed to do his duty so well was largely due to the influence of his queen, a fact he himself acknowledged. Also widely accepted as due largely to the Queen Mother's influence is the intransigent refusal to recognise the ex-King and his wife, afterwards styled the Duke and Duchess of Windsor. To the days of their deaths, the Duke and Duchess of Windsor were kept outside the royal circle and, except on brief visits, outside Britain. The Queen Mother later remarked that the strains of kingship hastened the death of her husband. Doubtless she blamed the Windsors for the fact.

Almost as soon as the Abdication Crisis was over, the Second World War began. The strain on both King and Queen were enormous. Not only was the king involved in matters of state, he was also needed for morale boosting trips to troops and bomb sites. In the early months of 1940 the East End and other industrial areas were heavily bombed. The royal couple visited many areas, but some locals resented the apparent privilege of royalty and were not slow in showing their feelings. In September a German plane rained bombs on Buckingham Palace, blasting sections apart. 'I'm glad we've been bombed,' said the Queen. 'It makes me feel I can look the East End in the face.'

The rest of the war was a constant strain with the Queen carrying out seemingly endless duties and encouraging her two daughters to undertake war work. In the fighting the Queen lost both a nephew and a brother-in-law, but the coming of peace marked a brief return to happier days. Princess Elizabeth was clearly very much in love with the dashing young naval officer Prince Philip. The Queen was at first reluctant to allow her daughter and heiress to the throne to marry at the young age of 21, but later relented and the wedding took place in November 1947.

Within a year of the wedding the health of the king was causing serious concern. His blood circulation was not as good as it should have been and led to fears of gangrene in one leg. In 1951 he was found to have lung cancer, which was operated on at once, but without success. In 1952, after years of watching her husband become progressively sicker, the Queen watched him die.

For several months the Queen Mother retired from public view with her grief. The coronation of her daughter again brought her out on a magnificent public occasion and many people commented on how well she looked. Before long the future pattern of her life had been set. Leaving Buckingham Palace, the Queen Mother established herself at Clarence House in the Mall. She bought a delapidated Castle of Mey in a remote glen of the Scottish Highlands and restored it. An interest in national hunt racing appeared with the Queen Mother buying and breeding a string of horses which have brought her mixed fortunes.

To the present day the unstinting devotion to duty of the Queen Mother has continued. To the public she has been a tireless patron of deserving societies and charities. She has also become established as 'the nation's favourite granny' through her constant devotion to her family. When her daughter and Prince Philip were absent on long official tours during the 1950s she cared for the young Prince Charles and Princess Anne at Clarence House. It was to Clarence House that Princess Margaret came for her first confinement.

More recently she looked after her eldest grandson's fiancee during the weeks leading up the wedding. It was from the Queen Mother that the young Lady Diana Spencer learnt the skills of tact and devotion necessary of a royal wife. After all, the Queen mother had been in very much the same situation as Lady Diana some sixty years earlier. Soon afterwards Sarah Ferguson also came to Clarence House in the build up to her wedding to Prince Andrew. Perhaps that marriage stirred more memories for the Queen Mother. The vivacious red-haired Sarah was about to marry a second son of the reigning monarch and take the title of Duchess of York, the same title the Queen Mother had held for so many years.

The Queen Mother has been a popular figure with the crowds ever since she joined the Royal Family by marrying the then Duke of York nearly 60 years ago. Wherever she appears the public treat her with affection. *Left:* The Queen and Queen Mother collecting flowers from well wishers after leaving church at Sandringham in August 1985. *Bottom left:* The Queen Mother attending the Sandringham Flower Show in 1985. *Below:* The Queen Mother outside Clarence House on 4th August 1987 when she mingled with the large crowd of well-wishers which had gathered to help celebrate her 87th birthday. *Bottom right:* The Queen Mother chats happily with youngsters who gathered outside the gates to Clarence House in the Mall to wish her a happy 89th birthday on 4th August 1989. *Facing page:* The Queen Mother emerges from Clarence House to welcome well-wishers on the occasion of her 88th birthday.

Horse racing is known as 'the sport of kings' and has become a firm favourite with the Queen Mother during her long years of widowhood. She owns a number of racehorses and avidly follows the events of the turf. Facing page: The Queen Mother and Diana, Princess of Wales, on the balcony of the Royal Box at Epsom Races on Derby Day 1986. Left: Prince Charles, in the formal dress demanded by the occasion joins his wife and grandmother on the balcony of the Royal Box at Epsom Races on Derby Day 1986. Below left: The Queen Mother chatting with Princess Michael of Kent on the balcony of the Royal Box at Epsom Races during Derby Day 1988. Bottom left: The Queen Mother is joined by her daughter, the Queen, and her grand-daughter, Princess Anne, for Derby Day 1988. Below: The Queen and Queen Mother discuss a horse in the paddock on Derby Day 1988.

Facing page: The Queen Mother relaxes on a wicker chair during a summer garden party. The Queen Mother's distinctive style of dress, characterised by flowing floral dresses and relaxed poise is ideally suited to summer days and warm weather clothing. Top: The Trooping the Colour ceremony of 1985 brought the Royal Family on to the balcony of Buckingham Palace in force. From left to right: Prince Michael of Kent, the Queen Mother, Prince Philip, The Queen, Princess Anne, Prince Charles, Princess Alice of Gloucester and Princess Diana holding young Prince Harry. Left: The Queen Mother celebrating her 84th birthday. Above: The Queen Mother, Princess Diana and Prince William on their way to the Trooping the Colour.

Top left: The Queen Mother holds a bunch of carnations up to the crowd while talking to well-wishers outside Clarence House on her 87th birthday. Top right: The Queen Mother waves from the balcony of Clarence House on her birthday in 1985. Left: The Queen Mother on the balcony of Clarence House on her 89th birthday. Above: A corgi with the Queen Mother at Clarence House while she celebrates her birthday in 1987. Facing page: The Queen Mother emerges from Clarence House on her birthday in 1988 accompanied by the Queen, Viscount Linley and Lady Sarah Armstrong-Jones.

Previous pages: The Royal Family gathers at Clarence House for lunch on the Queen Mother's birthday in 1989. Top: The Queen Mother accompanied by the Duchess of York, strolls through the crowd of race-goers at Royal Ascot in June 1986. Left: Princess Diana arrives with the Queen Mother at the Trooping the Colour in 1988. Above: The Queen Mother arrives at Ascot 1989. Facing page top: The Royal Family on the prestigious Derby Day 1987. Facing page bottom: The Queen Mother arrives with Princess Diana at Ascot in 1988.

Top: The Queen Mother inspects the 42nd Black Watch in full parade dress during her July 1987 visit to Berlin. Scottish regiments once fought in kilts but today wear them only on ceremonial occasions. Above: The Queen Mother attends a gala performance at Drury Lane in 1985. Right: Prince Charles and the Queen Mother in their formal robes as Knights of the Garter attending the Annual Service at Windsor in 1987. Facing page: The Queen Mother visiting the 1st Queen's Dragoon Guards at Saffron Walden.

Right: The Queen Mother emerges from Clarence House to meet the crowd on the occasion of her 89th birthday on 4th August 1989. Far right: A group of children allowed through the security cordon, present birthday gifts to the Queen Mother in 1989. Below: A quartet of royal ladies, the Queen Mother, Princess Margaret, the Princess of Wales and the Duchess of York stroll out of Clarence House to meet the crowds on the Queen Mother's birthday in 1986. Below right and facing page: The Queen Mother smiling at well-wishers on her birthday in 1989. The Queen Mother's vitality and charm are a wonder to all, especially when it is remembered that she was born in the year 1900 and is therefore the last surviving member of the Royal Family to have been born in the reign of Queen Victoria.

These pages: The Royal Family gathered together in August 1985 in order to celebrate the Queen Mother's 85th birthday. The gathering was held at the country residence of Sandringham and involved attendance at a religious service in the local parish church. As usual the Queen Mother was in the forefront of the members of the Royal Family meeting the public, accepting numerous small gifts of flowers and other trifles from an adoring circle of children and other admirers. The journey to Sandringham did not of course interfere with the by now traditional appearance of the Queen Mother to London well-wishers at Clarence House in the Mall.

Facing page: The Queen Mother at RAF Marham presenting new colours to the RAF Regiment which has responsiblity for defending RAF bases from ground attack. Top left: The Queen Mother strolls through the crowds at the Sandringham Flower Show . Top right: The Queen Mother emerging from Clarence House on her way to an official engagement. Despite her age the Queen Mother continues to attend a full programme of events. Left: The Queen Mother waves farewell to the crowd before re-entering Clarence House on her 86th birthday. Above: The Queen and Queen Mother outside Clarence House on the Queen Mother's birthday in 1989.

Facing page: The Queen Mother holding birthday cards and bouquets of flowers collected from the crowd outside Clarence House on her 86th birthday on 4th August 1986. Left: The Queen Mother walks across the paddock at Epsom Racecourse on Derby Day 1989. Below: The Queen Mother arrives to applause amid a sea of top hats and fashionably dressed ladies at Ascot in 1985. Bottom left: The Queen Mother arrives at Ascot in 1986 escorted by the then Sarah Ferguson who would soon become Duchess of York upon her marriage to Prince Andrew. During the engagement the future Duchess stayed with the Queen Mother so as to avoid the unwarranted attentions of the press. Bottom right: The Queen Mother, Princess Anne and Princess Margaret at Ascot in 1988.

Top left: The Queen Mother visits a youth club on the island of Jersey during a visit to the Channel Islands. Top right: The Queen Mother braves inclement August weather to meet a crowd of visitors while attending a church service at Sandringham on the occasion of her 85th birthday. Above: The Queen Mother is confronted by a prize-winning cow while chatting to the proud breeder at the annual Smithfield Show. Right: The Queen Mother pulling a pint of Youngs Bitter at a much-publicised visit to the London pub the Star.

This page: In August 1985 the Queen Mother, the longest surviving Victorian of the Royal Family, took a trip on the most modern of technology when she flew on an exhibition flight on Concorde, the supersonic passenger jetliner which is the pride of the British Airways fleet of aircraft, more often used by international businessmen. The Queen Mother was accompanied on the flight by her grandchildren Lady Sarah Armstrong-Jones and her brother Viscount Linley and by Miss Susannah Constantine.

Facing page top: The Queen Mother arrives in formal evening wear, complete with jewelled tiara, at the 1984 Royal Variety Performance accompanied by the Prince and Princess of Wales. Facing page bottom left: The Queen Mother holding the customary gifts of cards and flowers collected from well-wishers outside Clarence House on her 89th birthday. Facing page bottom right: The Queen Mother attends a service at the Wilkins Memorial dressed in mourning black, relieved only by the sparkle of diamonds and the lustre of pearls. Left: The Queen Mother sporting a red poppy on her black coat at the service on the Field of Remembrance. Below left: The Queen Mother carrying a union jack among the more usual flowers presented to her by the crowd outside Clarence House on her birthday. Below right: The Queen Mother holds some notes during a visit to Queen Charlotte's Hospital.

Top left: The Queen Mother dressed in a vivid yellow evening gown at the 1985 Royal Variety Performance. Top right: The Queen Mother dressed in her customary tiara and a flowing gown arrives for the premiere of Madame Souzatska followed by Princess Margaret. Above: The Queen Mother in a lace-enhanced gown shakes hands with the Australian pop-star Kylie Minogue. Right: The Queen Mother attending a performance at the Barbican in a startling gown of electric blue. Facing page: The Queen Mother appears again in the yellow gown previously worn to the Royal Variety Performance.

Facing page: The Queen Mother at the premier of Madame Souzatska with a glittering collection of jewels and an elegantly embossed clutch-bag. Top: The Queen Mother poses with the pilots of the Red Devils, the RAF's crack team of display pilots who perform dare-devil aerobatics at air shows in their red jets. Above: The Queen Mother jokingly pats the muzzle of a horse of the 1st Queen's Dragoon Guards which had tried to eat her bouquet of flower during a visit to the regiment's barracks. Right: The Queen Mother with the Irish wolfhound which is the regimental mascot of the Irish Guards while on a formal visit to the regiment. The bright red coats of British infantry regiments are today worn only on ceremonial occasions.

Below: The Queen and Prince Philip drive through a packed stadium in an open-topped landrover while on tour in Australia. It was in Australia that the informal Royal ritual known as the walkabout was first performed. At first the walkabout, strolling through the crowd to stop and chat here and there, was entirely unplanned and unprepared for in the itinery but it is now scheduled in to the time-table for most royal visits. The term is borrowed from the Australian word for an aimless wandering to see the sights. Right: The Queen waves to a crowd which gathered to watch her while on an official visit to Birmingham in 1989. Bottom left: The Queen in a rich outfit of matching coat and hat on walkabout. Bottom right: The Queen arriving at the Royal Box at Epsom for Derby Day 1989.

Top: The Queen, Queen Mother and the Prince and Princess of Wales in Scottish dress for the 1988 Braemar Games. The Royal connection with Braemar dates back to the time of Queen Victoria when she and Prince Albert first bought nearby Balmoral Castle as a Highland hunting lodge. The visit to Braemar forms part of an annual summer break in Scotland. Above: The Queen opening the restored crypt of St John's Church at Waterloo in 1984. Right: The Queen and Prince William at the Easter Service at Windsor.

Left: The Queen with ex-President Ronald Reagan of the United States at Buckingham Palace in 1989 when the American statesman visited Britain to receive an honorary knighthood following the end of his term of office in Washington. Below left: The Queen with ex-President Reagan and his wife Nancy. Below: The Queen processing to the annual Order of the Garter Ceremony in June 1986. The Most Noble Order of the Garter dates back to the 14th century when King Edward III instituted an order of knighthood which was intended to comprise the most honourable and valiant knights in Christendom. Facing page top: The Royal Family waves to the public from the balcony of Buckingham Palace in 1988. Facing page bottom: The Queen moves through the Royal Enclosure on her way to the Royal Box at Ascot in 1985.

Previous pages: The massed ranks of the Guards regiments escort the Queen along the Mall after the Trooping the Colour in 1988.
Facing page: The Queen taking the salute from the Guards as they march past during the Trooping the Colour ceremony of 1985. Top: The Royal Family on the balcony of Buckingham Palace after the 1985 Trooping the Colour Ceremony.
Above: The Queen leads the Royal Dukes and high ranking officers out of Buckingham Palace on route to Horse Guards for the 1985 Trooping the Colour Ceremony. Right: The Queen rides into Horse Guards in 1985. The Trooping the Colour ceremony had its origins over 300 years ago when flags or 'colours' formed rallying points for soldiers in the smoke of battle. The flags were trooped to ensure that each soldier knew them.

Facing page: The Queen at the official opening of the new British High Commission in Kuala Lumpa, the capital city of Malaysia, in October 1989 which she attended as part of an official tour of Far Eastern nations. Official tours such as this are usually arranged many months, if not years, in advance and it is only sometimes that they can be altered to include such engagements as this. More usually formal visits follow a set pattern of state occasions and receptions mixed with a few cultural breaks, such as visits to state operas or displays of traditional dancing. Left: The Queen and Queen Mother at Epsom Racecourse for the Derby in 1988. Below left: The Queen at Buckingham Palace in 1988. Below: The Queen pauses to smile at the crowd during an official visit to Matlock, in Derbyshire, in March 1985.

Facing page: The Queen resplendent in formal gown and jewels hosts a state banquet on board HM Yacht Britannia off Singapore in October 1989. Top: The Queen and Prince Philip at the 1989 Maundy Service which was held at Birmingham, following the tradition of changing venue each year. Above: The Queen attends a state banquet in Kuala Lumpa, in October 1989. Right: The Queen reading a speech during a state banquet held in Singapore in October 1989 as part of her official tour of Far Eastern countries.

Facing page: An official portrait of the Queen in relaxed and informal mood with a tweed skirt and casual cardigan. The picture was taken by Prince Andrew who, when his naval duties allow, is a keen amateur photographer. Right: The Queen keeps an eye on her young grandchildren, Prince William and Prince Harry, during an exciting polo match held at Windsor in June 1987. Below: The Queen waves a cheerful greeting to onlookers in Singapore's Chinatown during the official visit of October 1989. Below right: Princess Margaret, the Prince and Princess of Wales, the Queen and Prince Philip on the balcony of Buckingham Palace in 1989. Bottom right: The Queen and a top-hat wearing Prince Philip arrive at Ascot in 1985 for the traditional Royal Drive along part of the racecourse in front of the Grandstand.

Left: Prince Philip leans on his car to watch the progress of the carriage driving event at the Windsor Horse Show of 1985. Below: Prince Philip in the Carriage Driving event. Marks are awarded for the turn-out of the carriage and horses as well as for driving skill. Bottom left: The Queen, wrapped against a chill wind, watches Prince Philip as he drives his four-in-hand on the cross-country course. Bottom right: The Queen and Prince Philip turn to watch a passing horse at Epsom Races on Derby Day 1989.

Top: Prince Philip driving a magnificently turned-out four-in-hand carriage across the sands of Morecombe Bay in 1985. Above: The Queen and Prince Philip stroll along the Great Wall of China. The Wall was begun about 2,200 years ago and has been rebuilt many times since as a defence measure against the northern barbarians who periodically raided the settled farmlands of northern China. Right: Prince Philip steps on to the floored pavilion while the Queen pauses to watch an event at the Braemar Games of 1986.

Right: The Queen and Prince Philip lean on the balustrade of the Royal Box at the Epsom Racecourse to watch the progress of a race on Derby Day 1989. Below: Prince Edward shoulders his rifle before setting out on a long and gruelling route march as part of his training to be an officer in the Royal Marines. Below right: The Queen Mother accompanied by Prince Edward drives through the streets of London on her way to attend the marriage of her grandson Prince Charles to Lady Diana Spencer on 29th July 1981. Bottom right: Prince Edward, the most artistic and theatrically-minded of the Royal Family goes back-stage to visit the stars and other players of a show in 1988. Prince Edward joined the staff of the Really Useful Theatre Company so that he could become involved full-time in the theatre world.

Below: Princess Anne and her brother Prince Andrew at a Celebrity Charity Clay Pigeon Shoot at Chester in July 1984. Shooting has been a royal activity for many centuries. It was during a hunt with bows that King William II was killed in the New Forest in the year 1100 and many later monarchs spent their leisure time shooting. King Edward VII, when Prince of Wales, was a famous shot. The clay pigeon shoot has gained in popularity in recent years for not only is it cheaper than game shooting but does not involve the death of any animals. Right: Prince Edward arriving at London's Guildhall for a wine-tasting evening. Bottom left: Prince Edward in a casual jumper. Bottom right: The Windsor Horse Show in 1988.

Above: Princess Margaret attending the first day of the 1989 Chelsea Flower Show. Above right: Princess Margaret in a stunning red evening dress for a gala night at the Covent Garden Opera. Right: Princess Margaret arriving for the Children's Royal Variety Performance. Far right: Princess Margaret in a vivid green light evening gown arrives at a London theatre for an evening's entertainment. Facing page: Princess Margaret arriving for a performance of South Pacific in a rich blue satin gown and diamond jewellery. Princess Margaret is without doubt the greatest patron of the arts in the modern Royal Family and attends a great many plays and operas. Her interest extends beyond being a member of the audience and she is well-known for taking part in impromptu performances at small private parties.

Facing page: Princess Margaret at the British Television Awards ceremony on 8th April 1985. Top left: Lady Sarah Armstrong-Jones leaving the Oxfam Ball in the early hours of the morning of 5th December 1984 after attending the charity spectacular. Top right: Princess Margaret arriving at London's Barbican Theatre in April 1983. Left: Princess Margaret escorted by Lord Lonsdale arrives at the Royal Caledonian Ball. Above: Princess Margaret arrives at Ascot in 1986 accompanied by Sarah Ferguson.

These pages: Photographs taken during the visit to China by Princess Margaret and her two children Viscount Linley and Lady Sarah Armstrong-Jones in May 1987. Facing page: Princess Margaret receives a bouquet of flowers on arrival at Peking Airport. Right: Princess Margaret strolls along the top of a restored section of the Great Wall of China accompanied by translators and soldiers. Far right: The Royal visitors in the Forbidden City. Below: Princess Margaret flanked by her children and by Chinese ladies in traditional court dress. Bottom left: Viscount Linley and Lady Sarah lean on the parapet of the Great Wall of China. Bottom right: Lady Sarah Armstrong-Jones and Viscount Linley at the gateway to the Forbidden City, the royal apartments once kept hidden from westerners by the Chinese Emperors.

Facing page top: Prince Charles watches his sons, Prince William and Prince Harry, play along the stony banks of the River Dee on the Balmoral Estate during a short holiday in April 1987. Facing page centre left: Prince Charles leads his son on a fishing trip on the Dee in August 1987. Facing page bottom left and facing page bottom right: Prince Charles crosses a precarious rope bridge on the lower slopes of Ben Nevis with members of the Lochabar Mountain Rescue Team in August 1987. Top and left: Prince Charles fishing in the River Dee on the Balmoral Estate in May 1984. Above: Prince Charles returns to fish the same stretch of the Dee in September 1988.

Facing page top: Prince Charles gallops for the ball during a polo match at Cowdray Park Polo Club at Midhurst in July 1988. Left: Prince Charles's polo pony misses its footing sending the Prince rolling on the ground (above). Fortunately he was unhurt by his tumble. Facing page top left: Prince Charles playing for the Blue Devils at the Guards Club. Facing page top right: Changing shirts before a match at the Guards Club. Facing page bottom left: Prince Charles playing at the Palm Beach Polo Club during the 1985 Royal tour of the United States. Facing page bottom right: Prince Charles at the Guards Club.

Top: Prince Charles plays polo in Oman during the November 1986 Royal tour. Above: The Queen presents a polo trophy at the Guards Club, Windsor. Right: Prince Charles gallops into action at the Guards Club. Facing page: Prince Charles rides from a match at the Guards Club. Polo was originally an Indian game which was picked up by British officers and planters under the name of hockey, though the original name came back into common usage by about 1880.

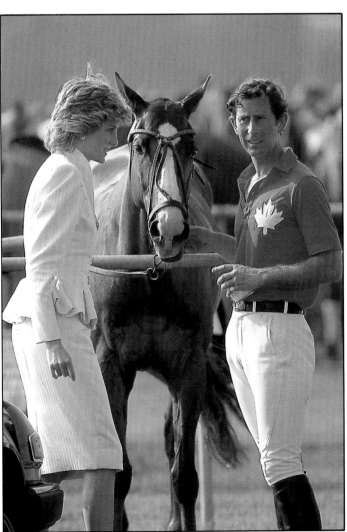

Facing page top: Prince Charles at the Cirencester Polo Club in May 1989. Facing page bottom left: Princess Anne congratulates Prince Charles after a win at the Cirencester Polo Club in June 1988. Facing page bottom right: Prince Charles and Prince William at Windsor Polo field in June 1987. Top left: Prince Charles receives a prize at the Guards Club in June 1988. Top right: The Prince and Princess of Wales on the polo field. Left: The Prince and Princess of Wales at the Guards Club in June 1986. Above: The Prince of Wales claims a kiss from his wife after receiving a winning trophy from her at the Guards Club in Windsor.

Above left: Prince Charles on an official visit to the war graves at Anzio in Italy, scene of massive Allied sea-bourne landings during the push for Rome in the Second World War. Above: Prince Charles visits Royal Naval vessels on escort duties in the Arabian Gulf during a tour of the Gulf States in 1989. Far left: Prince Charles at Tidworth Barracks. Left: Prince Charles prepares to fire a mortar during a visit to British troops on manoeuvre near Paderhorn in Germany. Facing page top: Prince Charles drives a tank on cross-country manoeuvres under the close supervision of the vehicle's usual driver while visiting troops in Germany. Facing page bottom left: Prince Charles talks to cheerful troops dressed in incongruous snow camouflage uniforms in Germany. Alpine troops are specially trained in mountain warfare in snow-bound conditions. Facing page bottom right: Prince Charles at Tidworth.

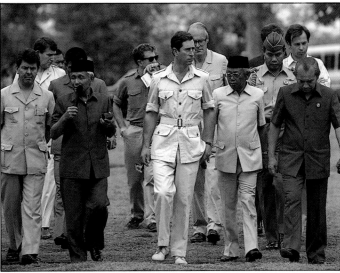

Facing page top: Prince Charles inspects the Kings Troop, Royal Horse Artillery, at St John's Wood Barracks in 1985. The Kings Troop were formed as a ceremonial battery when the Royal Artillery were abandoning horses in favour of motorised transport in the years after the First World War. Facing page bottom: Prince Charles with an escort of traditionally robed Arabs during his tour of the Gulf States in 1989. Top: Prince Charles inspects a guard of honour with the Emir of Bahrain on arrival in Bahrain during the 1989 tour of the Gulf States. Above: Prince Charles being shown around an ancient temple in Indonesia by an official guide. Right: Prince Charles in Australia on an official Royal tour in 1988.

Top: Prince Charles on a visit to Liverpool Football Club in May 1989 after the Hillsborough disaster in which nearly one hundred Liverpool fans were crushed to death when the crowd surged forward at Hillsborough football stadium during a match in an FA Cup qualifying round. Above: Prince Charles at the controls of his Wessex helicopter. Prince Charles is able to control a number of vehicles on the ground, on the water or in the air. Right: Prince Charles touring a Tornado aircraft factory in Germany.

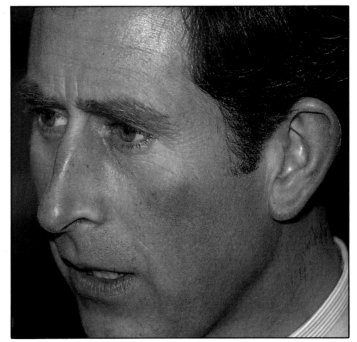

Top: Prince Charles chats to a group of forest rangers who have the demanding task of controlling poaching and illegal felling of trees in Cameroon's rain forests, a vital part of the ecology of East Africa. Left: Prince Charles holds the model Tornado aircraft presented to him during his tour of the German factory where the strike jet is manufactured. Above: Prince Charles has a technical point explained to him during his tour of the Tornado jet factory.

Top left: Prince Charles wearing the regimental tie of one of the many army formations with which he is associated. Top right: Prince Charles in contemplative mood as he pauses while sketching the countryside. Prince Charles is an accomplished amateur in watercolours and has achieved some success. One of his smaller landscapes was exhibited at the Royal Academy Summer Exhibition. Above: Prince Charles with the Queen and Prince Philip at Sandringham in January 1988. Right: Prince Charles in the robes of a Knight of the Bath at Westminster Abbey. The Most Honourable Order of the Bath was instituted in 1399 but fell into abeyance and was restored in 1725. Facing page: Prince Charles in a windcheater to protect himself against the bitter east wind in Norfolk.

This page: The wedding of Prince Charles to Lady Diana Spencer on 29th July 1981 made headline news around the world with hundreds of millions of viewers following events on their television screens. Top left: Lady Diana Spencer leaving Clarence House, where she had stayed during her engagement, accompanied by her father Earl Spencer. The glass carriage revealed something of the dress to the crowds which lined the route, but when Lady Diana descended from the carriage it was seen in its full glory. Above and left: Prince Charles and his bride travel back to Buckingham Palace in an open landau after the wedding. Above left: Prince Charles and the new Princess of Wales appeared on the balcony of Buckingham Palace after the ceremony to be greeted by the cheers of the many thousands of people who packed the Mall.

Top left: The new Princess of Wales attends a Christmas carol concert at Guildford Cathedral only a few months after her marriage to the Prince of Wales. Top right: The Princess of Wales dressed in sober black for her historic meeting with the Pope in the Vatican in 1985. Above: The Prince and Princess of Wales leaving St Mary's Hospital, Paddington, in 1982 carrying their first son, Prince William. The speed with which the Wales's began their family confirmed in the public's mind what had been suspected for some time, that the new Princess was extremely fond of children and was keen to have one of her own as soon as possible. Right: The Princess of Wales attending the 1984 Royal Variety Performance, the annual charity gala which is attended by at least one member of the Royal family.

Since their marriage in 1981 the Prince and Princess of Wales have undertaken a large number of foreign tours. These goodwill visits inevitably involve a large amount of hard work. Not only are the official events tiring in themselves, but the Princess must be continually thinking about her wardrobe. She is expected to appear in fashionable and stylish clothes at every occasion and to be immaculately turned out. This means that each function involves some hours of planning and preparation in advance. The Princess has shown herself to be an expert in such matters as was shown in Spain (below); in Melbourne, Australia (right); in Portugal (bottom left) and in Nigeria (bottom right).

Princess Diana has become an acknowledged leader of fashion. Her style has matured over the years from the shy, reserved Sloane Ranger image which she had when the engagement was first announced through to the sophisticated and chic impression which she creates today. In part the change has been due to the fact that as Princess of Wales she can and is expected to spend more on clothes than when she was simply Lady Diana, but the role she now plays in international fashion is mainly based on her own taste in clothes which is widely recognised as being sound and consistent. Far left: Princess Diana attending a gala night at the Coliseum. Left: The Prince and Princess of Wales dancing in 1988. Below left: Princess Diana in Cambridge. Below: Princess Diana appears at British Fashion Week.

Top left: Princess Diana attends the Remembrance Ceremony in Paris in November 1988. Top right: The Princess of Wales in Abu-Dhabi in March 1989. Left: Princess Diana in unusual male-style fashion opens the Glasgow Garden Festival in April 1988. Above: Princess Diana in Kuwait in March 1989. When visiting Islamic nations Royal ladies have to be careful not to offend the strict Moslem codes of female attire by covering their legs and arms as much as possible.

Top left: Princess Diana in Hyde Park in 1988. Top right: The Princess of Wales on an official visit to New York in February 1989. Journeys to the United States have become frequent events for the Prince and Princess of Wales. Above: A sunny smile from Princess Diana in Melbourne, the capital of Victoria in Australia, in January 1987. Right: Princess Diana takes on a distinctly oriental style while visiting Thailand in February 1988.

Far left: In November 1985 Princess Diana attended the premiere of the movie Santa Claus which starred the British actor Dudley Moore in the role of a hapless elf caught up in the frantic preparations for Christmas by Santa Claus. The eye-catching evening dress impressed many fashion commentators. Left: Princess Diana attends a state occasion in an elegantly cut evening gown during the Wales's tour of Germany. Below: Princess Diana in a wide-brimmed hat in Cameroon in March 1990. The hat style featured several times on this visit and may have been prompted by the searing heat of the African sun. Facing page top: Princes Diana chats with a dance troupe after watching a display of traditional tribal dances in Nigeria. Facing page bottom: Princess Diana talks informally to shoppers and stall-holders at a traditional women's craft market in the Nigerian city of Lagos.

Top left: Princess Diana attending a reception at the British Embassy in Paris during the tour of the French Capital in November 1988. Top right: Princess Diana is greeted by traditionally robed Arab dignitaries in Kuwait during a tour of Middle East nations in March 1989. Left: A startling pink evening gown was chosen by Princess Diana for an official banquet at Palm Beach in Florida. Above: Princess Diana shows off the stylish train of her evening gown while dancing in Melbourne, Australia, in January 1988. Facing page: Princess Diana in Kuwait in March 1989.

Top left: Princess Diana revived a fashion accessory from a past century when she used a muff to protect her hands in the chill wind of Basingstoke in April 1986. Though muffs can be useful not only for protection from the elements but also as a substitute handbag, the idea failed to catch on with the public, unlike so many other of Princess Diana's fashion innovations. Top right: Princess Diana in a smart two-piece tartan suit during her November 1988 visit to Paris. Left: Princess Diana in a simple white outfit for a polo match at Windsor in July 1986. Above: A broad brimmed hat suitable for hot climates was worn during an official tour of Gulf States.

Below: Princess Diana chose this stunning hat for a visit to Newcastle in May 1985. Not only did the hat catch the eye because of its bold colouring but also because the wide brim sprang from above the base line of the crown of the hat. Right: Princess Diana in an off-the shoulder gown of colourfully striped material which is carefully matched by the flowers in the bouquet. Bottom left: Princess Diana in a boldly patterned dress for the tour of the Middle East in 1989. Bottom right: Princess Diana in Toledo, one of the oldest towns in Spain. The British Royal family has important links with the Spanish Royal dynasty which regained its throne on the death of General Franco and introduced democracy.

In January 1985 the Prince and Princess of Wales travelled to Liechenstein as guests of the rulers of this tiny principality tucked away in the Alps between Austria and Switzerland. The ruling dynasty of the diminutive nation inhabits the castle of Vaduz (above) perched on a rocky crag high above the town of the same name. In the winter the slopes of Liechenstein become ideal sking territory and it was this that attracted the Royal couple.

Top left: *Princess Diana arrives at Aberdeen Airport for a visit to Balmoral in September 1986, accompanied by her two sons Prince William and Prince Harry. Top right: Princess Diana steps on to the tarmac at Aberdeen Airport in a windy squall with Prince Harry in September 1985. Above: Prince Harry's first day at Wetherby School in September 1989. Right: Princess Diana and Prince William are conducted around HMS Brazen in February 1986.*

Top left: In January 1987 Princess Diana talks to young Prince William before leading him into Wetherby School where he began his school career. Top right: Princess Diana and Prince Harry on their way to attend the traditional Easter Service held at Windsor in March 1989. Left: The two young princes, William and Harry, stride through the rain to watch their father play in a polo match held at Windsor in June 1987. Above: A smartly dressed Prince William at the Royal Family's Easter Service at Windsor in April 1988.

Below: A casually dressed Princess Diana races for the tape during the Mothers' Race at the annual Wetherby School Sports Day in June 1989. Right: Prince William trailing in a race at Wetherby School Sports Day in June 1989. Bottom left: Princess Diana, managing to look trendy as well as informal in jeans, sweat-shirt and jacket leads Prince William across the turf of Windsor Great Park to watch Prince Charles play in a polo match in May 1988. Bottom right: Princess Diana with identically dressed Prince William and Prince Harry arrives at Aberdeen Airport in August 1989. Facing page: Princess Diana and Prince Harry on holiday with King Juan Carlos of Spain on Majorca in August 1988.

Above left: Princess Diana inspects a smartly turned out Gurkha unit during the Sovereign's Day Parade at Sandhurst Military College. The Gurkhas are a military unit raised from among the hill tribes of Nepal in the Himalayas and employed by the British government as a historical hang-over from the days of the British Raj. Above right: Princess Diana talking to members of the guard at the Falklands Memorial Service in June 1985. Far left: Princess Diana struggles to control a flying skirt as she steps down from a helicopter of the Queen's Flight while arriving at Tiverton-upon-Avon in May 1985. Left: Princess Diana's first public appearance in uniform at the Red Cross service held in Bristol Cathedral in December 1984.

Right: Prince Charles and Princess Diana drive in an open-topped car around the site of the Battle of Bosworth Field in Leicestershire on the anniversary of the battle. It was at the battle, fought in 1485 that the Plantagenet Dynasty was overthrown and its last king, Richard III, slain by the troops of the Tudor claimant King Henry VII who took the throne. Below: Princess Diana chatting happily to soldiers of the Hampshire Regiment on manoeuvres in Germany. Bottom left: Princess Diana takes the controls of a light battle tank while inspecting the British Army of the Rhine in Germany. Below right: Princess Diana in a startling, star-spangled evening gown of midnight blue attends a formal banquet in Florence, Italy.

Facing page: Princess Diana in a smart navy blue and white dogtooth coat with navy hat while on tour in Germany in 1988. Top: Princess Diana moves through the crowded Royal Enclosure at Ascot in 1989. Left: Princess Diana at a polo match at the Guards Club in Windsor in July 1988. Above: Prince Charles and Princess Diana on the balcony of the Royal Box at the Epsom Racecourse on Derby Day 1986. The Epsom Derby has been one of the most prestigious flat horse races since it was first run over the short downland turf in 1780. The name comes from the Earl of Derby, who put up the prize for the first race and has been used by several other prestigious races around the world, such as the Kentucky Derby in the United States.

Below: Princess Diana watches while Prince Charles ceremonially dots the eye of a festive dragon on arrival in Hong Kong. Right: Princess Diana meeting Michael Chang, the tennis prodigy of the late 1980s when visiting the David Lloyd tennis centre in Raynes Park, London. Bottom left: Princess Diana chats to the crowd and gathers gifts of flowers while visiting a British military base in Hong Kong. Bottom right: Princess Diana being presented with garlands of flowers by the daughters of Gurkha soldiers stationed in Hong Kong during the controversial visit to the colony in 1989. The imminent negotiations between Britain and China concerning the hand over of Hong Kong to China in 1997 caused anxiety about the wisdom of the Royal tour, but in the event few disruptions occurred and the tour went ahead as planned.

The many duties of a Royal princess take Princess Diana to a great many places around the world and place her in varied situations. Yet at all times she must be dressed appropriately and show an interest in whatever is going on around her, unless arrangements begin to go wrong when tact of a high order is called for on her behalf. *Top left: Princess Diana visits the Royal Air* Force base at Scampton, near Lincoln, in July 1985. It was from this base that the famous dambuster raid was launched in May 1943. *Top right: Princess Diana visits Newcastle. Above: Princess Diana flanked by young girls in traditional formal dress while visiting Indonesia in 1989. Right: Princess Diana visits Hereford in April 1985.*

Far left: Princess Diana at Tiverton-upon-Avon near Bath.
Left: Princess Diana is greeted by Nancy Reagan on arriving in Washington D.C. for an official visit. The Reagans were the first family in the United States for eight years in the 1980s and so were hosts to several Royal visits to the American capital. In 1989 Ronald Reagan stepped down as President of the United States to be replaced by his Vice President George Bush. Below left: Princess Diana watches the progress of a polo match in which Prince Charles is playing at Windsor in June 1985. Prince Charles is an expert polo player and has long been interested in the more adventurous equestrian sports. Below: Princess Diana in Indonesia as part of an extended tour of Far Eastern countries in November 1989.

Below: Princess Diana in suitably modest clothing on the 1986 Royal tour of the Gulf States in 1986. Right: Princess Diana returned to the Middle East in 1989 where, among other official engagements, she visited a hospital to see how modern medical aids were being put to use. Bottom left: Princess Diana at the Elysee Palace in Paris in 1988 for a formal dinner with President Mitterand, head of state of France. Bottom right: Princess Diana adopts a loosely Arabian style for her clothing at a traditional desert banquet during the tour of the Middle East in 1989. The Arab peoples of the Gulf states are keenly aware of their desert heritage and have not allowed the modern wealth generated by oil to mask the impoverished background of desert nomads from which many of the most prominent families have sprung.

Below: Princess Diana in Indonesia in 1989. Right: The Princess of Wales in Newcastle in 1985. Bottom left: The Princess of Wales visits Redruth in Cornwall in April 1985. Bottom right: Princess Diana visiting the war graves cemeteries at Anzio in Italy in April 1985. The Anzio landings took place on 22nd January 1944 when 50,000 troops were landed 70 miles behind the German front line in Italy in an attempt to outflank and rout the Germans. Instead the American commander stayed put, allowing his forces to be surrounded by the Germans and heavily bombarded by enemy artillery.

Top left, top right and above: The Princess of Wales on the Royal tour of the Middle East in 1989. Relations between the British Royal family and the ruling dynasties of the desert states are extemely close. Most of the Arab Royal families are descended from desert tribesmen who fought for independence from the Ottoman Empire during the First World War and were aided by the British. Links between the emergent royals and Britain were retained after the fighting. Right: Princess Diana sports an unusual hat with ribbons dangling from beneath the brim for a visit to Madrid, Spain.

Top left: The Princess of Wales visits the La Spezia Naval Base in Italy in April 1985. Top right: The Prince and Princess of Wales in Sardinia. Left: Princess Diana pauses to talk to some children during a visit to Newham in London's East End in 1984. Above: The Prince and Princess of Wales enjoy a romantic gondola ride in Venice during their tour of Italy in May 1985. Gondolas are unique to Venice, where they are needed for commuting around the water-locked city. The origins of the gondola are lost in time, but they are clearly shown on paintings completed four centuries ago.

Below: Princess Diana presents a magnificent trophy to a polo team, which includes Prince Charles, which won a polo competition in Palm Beach, Florida, in 1985. Right: The Princess of Wales at Ascot in June 1985. Bottom left: Princess Diana applauds her husband's skill on a polo pony at Windsor in 1985. Bottom right: Prince Charles and Princess Diana with two very different forms of transport. The polo ponies belong to a previous era of horseback travel, though they are still used for sport, while the Aston-Martin open-topped sports car is very much a 20th century vehicle.

Top: Prince Charles and Princess Diana with their two sons, Prince William and Prince Harry on board HM Yacht Britannia off Venice in May 1985. Above: Prince William rides in a carriage with his great-grandmother the Queen Mother on his way to watching the Trooping the Colour ceremony in 1988. Right:

Prince Charles receives a polo trophy from his sister-in-law the Duchess of York in 1988. Facing page top: The Royal Family after the Trooping the Colour ceremony in 1989. Facing page bottom: The Royal Family on the balcony of Buckingham Palace.

Facing page: Princess Alexandra in full court dress attending a state banquet at the Guildhall in London to honour President Banda of Malawi during his state visit to Britain in April 1985. Top left: Princess Anne in formal dress for an official engagement in the Gambia in 1990. Top right: The Duchess of Gloucester at a reception at the Intercontinental Hotel in 1986. Although the Duke and Duchess of Gloucester are not on the Civil List and do not have to fulfil public engagements their involvement with many organisations ensures that they are kept busy. Left: Princess Alexandra in Hyde Park in February 1983. Above: The Duchess of Kent attending a Christmas Party of the Not Forgotten Association held at Buckingham Palace Mews. The Duchess of Kent is often said to be the best dressed of all the Royal ladies.

Facing page: Princess Anne in a severe, Puritan style collar at an event organised for the Butler Trust, one of many charitable organisations with which she is involved. Top left: Princess Anne in casual yet stylish clothing designed to keep her cool during an arduous visit to Africa on behalf of the Save the Children Fund, a charity with which she has become heavily involved in recent years. Top right: Princess Anne in more formal, but still relaxed, clothing for an event in the Gambia in 1990. Left: Princess Anne in Windsor. Above: Princess Anne helps her daughter Zara Phillips with riding skills at a gymkhana. Princess Anne is an accomplished horsewoman who has competed in many international equestrian events and has won a number of prestigious prizes.

Top left: Princess Anne confronts a heavily camouflaged soldier while visiting army manouevres at Warminster in September 1985. Top right: Princess Anne during a visit to the Royal Naval Museum at Portsmouth in February 1989. Left: Princess Anne trudges through thick mud, accompanied by senior officers, while attending army manoeuvres on the open countryside around the West Country town of Warminster.

Above: Princess Anne adjusts a pair of goggles before driving a light tank as part of the army manouevres held in Wiltshire in September 1985. Facing page top: Princess Anne and Captain Mark Phillips driving to the wedding of Prince Andrew and Sarah Ferguson. Facing page bottom: Princess Anne inspecting the troops on Sovereign's Day Parade at Sandhurst in April 1986.

Top left: Princess Anne and Captain Mark Phillips, walking on crutches after a minor accident, attend Newbury Races in May 1985. Top right: Princess Anne leaving the Royal Easter Service at Windsor when the Queen's immediate family traditionally gather together in April 1988. Left: Princess Anne visits Cambridge in June 1985. The university at Cambridge has traditionally educated Royal youngsters. Above: Captain Mark Phillips gallops away from an obstacle on the cross country event of the second day of the Three Day Event at Windsor Horse Trials in May 1985.

Far left: Peter Phillips, suitably dressed in lounge suit and tie leaves Sandringham Church after the Christmas service of December 1985. The royal home at Sandringham was a great favourite with King Edward VII who used it as a hunting lodge to which to invite his friends for informal weekends and shooting trips. It has since become traditional for the Royal family to gather at Sandringham for Christmas when the various generations of royalty engage in traditional games, such as charades, and exchange gifts around the Christmas tree, a custom introduced to this country by Prince Albert, direct ancestor of the Queen. Left: Princess Anne at Ascot in 1989. Below left: Princess Anne, in stylish evening wear arrives for a Royal Film Premiere. Below: Zara Phillips at the Stony Easton Horse Trials in March 1989.

Princess Anne's patronage of the Save the Children Fund has done a great deal to restore her popularity with the public at a time when her occasionally somewhat caustic remarks had made her one of the least favourite members of the Royal Family. The post has also involved the Princess Royal in a great deal of arduous foreign travel to areas noted only for their destitution or to war zones where other travellers might hesitate to tread. Top left: Princess Anne being shown around an historic temple in Rangoon, Burma, by traditionally clad Burmese guides. Top right and left: Princess Anne visits a camp of Cambodian refugees near the Thai border. Above: Princess Anne in the Bangkok slums.

The Princess Royal, in her role as patron of the Save the Children Fund undertakes perhaps more foreign tours than any other member of the Royal Family, and these are very much removed from the comfortable conditions of most Royal tours, or indeed those enjoyed by most holiday-makers. Due to the nature of its work, the fund operates in areas where disease and poverty are rife and it is to these that the Princess must travel. Right, bottom left and bottom right: The Princess Royal visits an up-river village in Gambia. This tiny republic encloses the banks of the Gambia River in West Africa and little else. It is entirely surrounded by Senegal, except at the coast, and is lacking in natural resources. Below: Princess Anne participating in a ritual at a Thai temple.

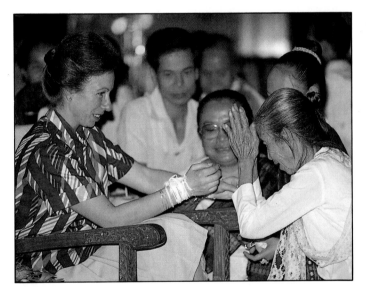

Princess Anne is a noted horsewoman who has won many trophies and championships. Facing page: Participating in the Aldon Horse Trials in 1986. Top left: Princess Anne with her son and the Queen at the Badminton Horse Trials in April 1983. Top right: Princess Anne in one of her rare outings as a jockey at the Epsom Races in April 1985. Above: Princess Anne rides through atrocious weather in the show jumping round of the Crookham Horse Trials in March 1988. Right: Princess Anne with her husband, Captain Mark Phillips, at the Windsor Horse Trials in May 1985.

Below: The Queen with Princess Anne and her two children, Peter and Zara Phillips, watch the progress of the Windsor Horse Show in May 1985. Right: Young Zara Phillips astride a pony at the Tidworth Horse Trials in 1987. Bottom left: Zara Phillips skips across the turf during one of the less exciting phases of the 1985 Windsor Horse Show. Bottom right: Princess Anne points out an incident to her children at the Windsor Horse Trials of 1985. Facing page top: Peter Phillips competing at the Windsor Horse Trials of 1989. Facing page bottom: Captain Mark Phillips encouraging his two children before they ride in the 1988 Aldon Horse Trials.

Peter Phillips has already shown that he is likely to follow his parents into the equestrian world of sport. Both his father and mother were competitors of an international standard at the time of their marriage and young Peter Phillips has competed in a number of junior events at horse trials. Left: Peter Phillips at the Stoney Easton Park Horse Trials in March 1989. He is also active in other sports as shown in the football match (above, top right and top left) staged at Port Regis School in September 1985.

Below: Peter and Zara Phillips at the Stoney Easton Park Horse Trials in March 1989. Right: Captain Mark Phillips and the Princess Royal at the Windsor Horse Trials in May 1988. Bottom left: Zara Phillips wriggles in her chair while Peter Phillips watches the progress of events at the Windsor Horse Trials in 1985. Bottom right: Princess Anne and her father, the Duke of Edinburgh, at Cambridge University in June 1985. The Royal Family has a long connection with Cambridge University for it is to Cambridge that princes have traditionally gone after education at school. Both Prince Charles and Prince Edward finished their formal education at Cambridge.

Top left: Princess Anne riding in the 1986 Aldon Horse Trials. Top right: Princess Anne riding over sticks at Newbury Races in March 1987. Members of the Royal Family rarely ride as jockeys in horse races, usually preferring to keep their equestrian outings confined to eventing and show-jumping, which are considered to be more suitable to their station and position. Centre right: Princess Anne arriving at Ascot in June 1985 with her grandmother, the Queen Mother. Above: Zara Phillips greets her mother at the Windsor Horse Trials in 1985. Right: The Princess Royal in a flowing summer gown with matching hat and shoes at Ascot in 1989.

Top left: Princess Anne rises from her shooting stick to follow a piece of the action at the 1989 Windsor Horse Trials. Top right: Princess Anne rides through the winter landscape at Sandringham in January 1984, leading a small pony by the bridle. Her two children, Peter and Zara, were encouraged to ride from an early age. All members of the immediate Royal Family need to learn to ride to a degree for many of the ceremonial occasions demand that they ride to or from the ceremony in procession. Left: Princess Anne at the Windsor Horse Trials in May 1988. Above: Princess Anne, accompanied by a dog, strides across the grounds at Sandringham in 1986.

The marriage of Prince Andrew to Sarah Ferguson was one of the most popular Royal occasions in recent years, bringing tens of thousands of people on to the streets of London to help celebrate the ceremony. The wedding took place on 23rd July 1986 and was attended by the pomp and circumstance usually reserved for such evetnts. Processions of carriages and mounted troopers in glittering uniforms passed along the streets before the groom and his supporter, Prince Edward, emerged from Buckingham Palace in an open landau (left) to drive to Westminster Abbey. After the ceremony the new Duke and Duchess of York emerged to the cheers and congratulations of the crowds (facing page) and then drove to Buckingham Palace for the wedding breakfast and to appear on the balcony with members of their families (above).

Previous page: Prince Andrew and his bride, Sarah, drive to Buckingham Palace after their wedding through a Mall lined with guards and packed with crowds of well-wishers. Top left: The Duke and Duchess of York stroll through water-gardens during their tour of Canada in 1989. Top right: The Duchess of York arriving in Venice on board a motor launch, probably the best way to approach the water-bound city for the best views are to be obtained from the surface of the lagoon in which the city stands. Above: The Duke and Duchess of York in rugged outdoor gear before setting off on a canoe journey during their 1987 tour of Canada. Right: The Duke and Duchess of York in Australia. The Duke wears his naval uniform for he still holds an active commission in the senior service.

Left: The Duke and Duchess of York stroll through the streets of Aberdeen. Bottom left: The Duchess of York at the start of the Whitbread Round the World Yacht Race. The Duke and Duchess of York in formal evening attire for an official function in Venice during their 1989 tour of Italy. The vivid evening gown worn by the Duchess is typical of the clothes she has favoured since marrying the Duke. She has shown a flair for experimentation with colours and fabrics which is not matched by the more conservative ladies of the Royal Family. Though this willingness to try new combinations sometimes leads to garments considered disasters by fashion commentators, it can also lead to truly stunning creations as that seen here and always keeps the pundits guessing.

Left: The Duke and Duchess of York visiting Mid-Glamorgan. The Duke is wearing his naval uniform, complete with the campaign medals he gained through service in the Falklands War of 1982. Below: The Duke of York bends to exchange words with the Duchess while she signs a visitors' book during their tour of Canada. Bottom left: Prince Andrew, garbed in practical yellow plastic oilskins, steers a yacht through a choppy sea. Bottom right: The Duchess of York in an unusual black leather jacket at the Savoy Hotel. Facing page top: The Duke and Duchess of York on board Britannia as it steams into Portsmouth at the end of their honeymoon. Facing page bottom: The Duchess of York chats to schoolchildren during a visit to Windlesham in Surrey.

Left: The Duchess of York laughs at a comment from the crowd during a walkabout in York. Below: Sarah Ferguson arrives at Ascot Racecourse in 1986. Bottom left: The Duchess of York and Princess of Wales on the ski slopes at Klosters in March 1988. Klosters is an Alpine resort which has been a favourite with the younger members of the Royal Family for some years. Bottom right: A sombre Princess of Wales, accompanied by the Duchess of York, returns to Britain from Klosters in March 1988 after the tragic accident in which Major Lindsay was killed when an avalanche almost overwhelmed the Royal party. Prince Charles came close to being killed in the incident and several others were injured.

Left: The Duke and Duchess of York talking to the well-known artist David Hockney at an exhibition of his work held in Los Angeles. The painting seen in the background is Hockney's work and might be considered typical of much of his output in recent years. The Duke and Duchess are perhaps best known as outdoor people with a liking for action and activity, but both have an artistic streak. Before her marriage the Duchess worked in publishing while the Duke has a flair for photography which he indulges whenever his duties allow. Bottom left: The Duchess of York in a fetching outfit of pink and black attends a function in California. Below: The sunshine brings a sunny smile to the face of the Duchess of York in Canada in July 1989.

Above: The Duchess of York receives a bouquet of summer flowers from a young girl while visiting Canada in July 1989. Top right: The Duchess of York in Canada in July 1989. Right: The Duke and Duchess of York wearing matching tartan kilt and skirt on a visit to Aberdeen in 1988. In common with all members of the Royal Family, the Duke and Duchess of York are entitled to wear the Royal Stuart clan tartan which is predominantly red, but they may also wear any of the non-clan tartans such as that worn here. Far right: The Duke of York helps the Duchess disembark from a boat while touring Canada in 1989. Facing page: The Duchess of York in formal attire, including a beautiful jewelled tiara, at a formal dinner during the Yorks' tour of Canada in the summer of 1989.

Facing page top: A sudden gust of wind causes the Duchess of York and Princess of Wales to hold on to their hats on the balcony of the Royal Box at Epsom Racecourse on Derby Day 1987. The Prince of Wales stands beside his wife.

Facing page bottom: The Duke and Duchess of York relax while watching a display during the Royal tour of Canada in July 1989.

Above: The Duchess of York in a summery, short-sleeved dress in Canada in 1989. Above right: The Duchess of York waves to cheering crowds during the Yorks' tour of Canada in July 1989. Right: The Duchess of York dressed in a fetching velvet-bodiced evening gown at a film premiere at the Odeon Marble Arch in March 1989. Far right: The Duchess of York on the Canadian tour of 1989.

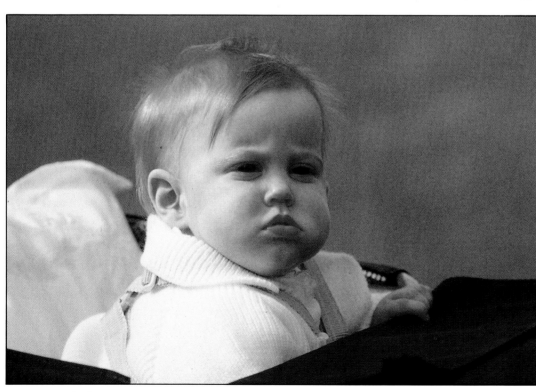

Above left: The Duke and Duchess of York leaving Great Portland Street Hospital with their first child, Princess Beatrice. Top right: The Duchess of York and the Princess of Wales in the Royal Box on the Centre Court at Wimbledon for the 1988 tennis championships. Both the Princess and the Duchess are keen tennis enthusiasts and returned to Wimbledon again in 1989 (above) to watch that year's championships. Left: Princess Beatrice looks up from her pram while on the way to meeting the Duke of York at Leith Docks when his ship, HMS Edinburgh docked in April 1989. Prince Andrew continues active service as helicopter pilot on board the naval ship and fits his official duties as a prince of the realm around his tours of duty on board ship.

Top left: The Duchess of York at a polo match in Windsor in June 1989. Top right: The Duchess of York awaiting her husband's ship at Portsmouth Docks in August 1989. Left: Prince Andrew, Duke of York, bends to receive a cute teddy bear dressed in regimental combat gear from the daughter of a British serviceman while visiting the British Army of the Rhine in Germany in July 1989. Even the army veterans watching the scene found it hard to suppress a chuckle. Above: Princess Beatrice playing in the snow while on holiday in Klosters in January 1990. Despite the fatal accident of March 1988, Klosters is still a favoured Royal ski resort.

Facing page: The Duke and Duchess of York attending a showing of White Mischief. The Duchess appeared in a flamboyant dress of black with heavily rouched salmon-pink satin sleeves which was nothing if not eye-catching. Top left: The Duke of York attends a function in naval overcoat during the Royal tour of Australia. Top right: The Duchess of York lifts Princess Beatrice from the snow during a holiday in Klosters in January 1990. Above: The Duchess of York holds securely on to Princess Beatrice on a tame toboggan ride in front of the press at Klosters in 1990. Right: Prince Andrew wearing kilt and sporran for a visit to Scotland.

Left: The Duke and Duchess of York with Princess Beatrice board HM Yacht at Portsmouth Docks on their way to Balmoral Castle for the traditional Royal summer break in August 1989. The summer holiday is enjoyed by most of the Queen's immediate family and allows them to gather together out of the public eye. Below left and facing page: The Duchess of York keeps tight hold of Princess Beatrice in April 1989 as she watches HMS Edinburgh steam into Leith Docks with Prince Andrew on board. Below: Prince Andrew holds his daughter after disembarking from his ship for a short leave with his family. Like many naval wives, the Duchess of York is separated from her husband for long periods of time while his ship is at sea and the reunions are highly emotional moments.

The approaching birth of a second child to the Duke and Duchess of York in early 1990 caused much speculation and excitement. When the Duchess was hurried into Great Portland Hospital in March the nation waited for news, which when it came revealed that a second daughter had been born. Members of the Royal family, (facing page bottom left) the Queen and (bottom right) the Princess of Wales, visited the hospital to the cheers of a small crowd which remained outside the hopsital. Left and bottom left: Princess Beatrice visited her new sister. Eventually the Duchess herself appeared with the child, by then named as Eugenie, held firmly in her arms (facing page top, facing page bottom right and below). Overleaf: The Duke and Duchess of York with their two daughters.